POWER WITHOUT GLORY

a Study in Ecumenical Politics

IAN HENDERSON

Power Without Glory

A STUDY IN ECUMENICAL POLITICS

JOHN KNOX PRESS
Richmond, Virginia

British edition published by Hutchinson & Co. Ltd., London, 1967
American edition published by John Knox Press, Richmond, Virginia, 1969

262.001
H38p
74853
August, 1971

Standard Book Number: 8042-1497-2
Library of Congress Catalog Card Number: 69-19857
© Ian Henderson 1967
Printed in the United States of America

This book is dedicated to the good Christians in every denomination who do not care greatly whether there is One Church or not

NOTE

IT was originally intended to print in the Appendix to Chapter 16, the Grey Document (A(E)P3) and certain extracts from the minutes of the Meetings of the Special Committee on 29th October 1965, and 26th November 1965.

After consultation with lawyers in both England and Scotland, it was decided that to do so in a British edition of the book could constitute a breach of the Copyright Act of 1956. These documents are in the possession of the author in view of his having been a member of the Special Committee, and material in them provides the basis for statements made in Chapters 16 and 17.

IAN HENDERSON
University of Glasgow

Contents

Author's Note

It is always pleasant to record one's indebtedness to other writers. The insights of men like E. H. Carr, Reinhold Niebuhr, Karl Jaspers, Hans-Georg Gadamer and Sir Halford Mackinder have contributed to make the writing of this book possible. In the actual writing, I have tried to avoid unnecessary technical terms and produce a work intelligible to the general reader.

Perhaps a personal note may be permitted. Disliking controversy, I was reluctant to write this book and put off doing so. I only began the manuscript after the Nottingham Declaration of 1964 had made it clear that the supporters of the Ecumenical Movement had high hopes of exterminating at a relatively early date all the churches in my country with the exception of one of which I would be conscientiously unable to be a member.

I hope that in my reaction to this situation I have not criticised anyone unfairly. The trick of passing a desire for power off as love is played wherever there is a possessive parent. If, as I argue, it is also found in the field of ecclesiastical politics, those who practise it there are, like possessive parents, unconscious of what they are doing and often very nice people indeed. The worst culprit is ecumenical language. Framed to conceal rather than describe events, it is admirably calculated to hide the actions of anyone who uses it from himself and to make it almost impossible for him to avoid double-think and double-talk.

I would like to thank the Rev. Iain Nicol and Mrs M. Usher of the Systematic Theology Department of this University for their help in preparing the manuscript for publication.

The University,
Glasgow.

Foreword

There are several contentions put forward in this book. The first is that the idea of the One Church, so far from providing a goal which all Christians are obliged to seek after, is, in fact, probably the worst idea which has ever influenced the minds of Christians. The true Christian position is not that God is One but that God is love. The imperative binding on all Christians is not to belong to one ecclesiastical organisation but to love their fellow Christians (and indeed everyone else) no matter what ecclesiastical organisation they belong to. In so far as the Ecumenical Movement has led Christians to do this more than they have done before, it is to be welcomed. No one in his senses can fail to rejoice in the thaw between Catholicism and Protestantism. If that were all that there was to the Ecumenical Movement then there would be no place for criticism of it.

But there is more to the Ecumenical Movement. There is, as far as I can see after discussion with the members of the Ecumenical party in my own church over a number of years, a failure to face up to the fact that Christians differ honestly from one another on intellectual matters and in all probability will continue to do so. You cannot remove sincere intellectual differences simply by saying that they ought not to exist. For as Kant reminded us long ago, 'ought' implies 'can'. And the trouble is that many Protestants find themselves quite unable to share the views of their Catholic or Anglican fellow-Christians, however much they would like to do so. It is not that the Protestant does not want to believe in Transubstantiation, for who could fail to be attracted by a doctrine which brings the Saviour so near? It is that he finds his mind refuses to work in terms of the Aristotelian metaphysic of substance and attribute on which the doctrine of Transubstantiation depends. Any Real Presence the Protestant is able to find in the Sacrament must rest on a different basis. But if that is so doctrinal unity cannot be an imperative and denominations which represent basic doctrinal differences cannot be sinful.

Another contention put forward in this book is that discussion about the Ecumenical Movement persistently fails to bring the factor of power into the open. This is perhaps a trend of our time. The Victorians tended not to talk about sex but that did not keep them from practising it. We in our day tend not to talk about power but that does not keep us from practising it. If politics is the art of the possible, then power forms an indispensable factor in all politics, including ecclesiastical politics. Certainly in the Church of Scotland, the Ecumenical Party stands out for its skill in seizing power in the form of convenerships, committee majorities and publicity. The story of how this was done and how the power has been used is told in Part III.

The important part which power plays in Ecumenical party politics leads one to ask whether it does not play an equally important part in the formation of Ecumenical concepts. In particular one must ask whether the oneness which is the basic concept of the Ecumenical Movement is an expression of power or of love. One must also ask, though this question is only briefly touched on in this book, how far orthodoxy is definable in terms of ecclesiastical power, or more specifically, how far a doctrine like that of apostolic succession is simply the expression of the power claims of an ecclesiastical class. These are the themes dealt with in Part I.

Power, of course, has played a part in the ecclesiastical world long before the rise of the Ecumenical Movement. For that reason I have written of Anglo-Scottish ecclesiastical relations from the Reformation onward. The factor of power supplies the key to many of the complexities in the past ecclesiastical relations between these two countries which are dealt with in Part II. If so, does it not provide a key to their relations in the present and the future? This question is rendered more acute by the loss of English power in the last fifty years. In a short space of time Englishmen have lost the power they once had to dominate the lives of millions of their fellow human beings. It would be unrealistic as well as unsympathetic to expect the adjustment to this loss of power to be easy. It is only natural to ask if, under cover of the Ecumenical Movement, compensation is being sought in part by the establishment of a new Anglican imperialism.

Finally there is the question whether those of us who cannot accept the assumptions of the Ecumenical Movement, must, in the event of its victory, allow ourselves to be driven out of the Christian Church.

I. H.

PART ONE

Introductory

I

The Flaw

WHY have Christians fallen out with one another so much? Right from the start they have been getting each other's back up. According to the gospels, the disciples quarrelled about who was to be Top Christian. According to the Epistle to the Galatians, St. Paul and St. Peter had what must have been a pretty unpleasant show down at Antioch. According to another of St. Paul's epistles, the Christians at Corinth went in for squabbles in a big way. And Professor Kaesemann, a leading New Testament specialist of today, maintains that the gospels were written because there was fairly strong disagreement among the early Christians as to what was genuine Christian preaching and what was not.[1]

One suspects that the heathen who marvelled at the way Christians loved one another didn't know them very well. Ironically and wistfully one finds oneself hoping that he never came to be one himself and so was able to retain his illusions. Otherwise he might well have become like the man who admires an outwardly united family and then marries into it to find it full of tensions and antipathies.

This is, of course, very sad. For Christianity is a revelation of love. It is the revelation that God so loved the world that He gave His only-begotten Son. And it is the injunction that Christians become one with Christ by giving themselves up to the love of God and their neighbour.

It is the fact that it is a gospel of love which makes Christianity

1. In his essay 'Sackgassen im Streit um den historischen Jesus' in 'Exegetische Versuche und Besinningungen Band 2' Göttingen 1964.

3

at once so difficult and so attractive. In a jungle or a concentration camp it is not easy to believe that this universe is in the
control of a Being whose nature is love; in a home or an office
or a factory it is not easy to love the extremely difficult person
with whom we are thrown into contact every day. No one with
any sense would disparage the difficulties in the Christian way
of love. It is no accident that its symbol is a Cross not a feather
bed. And yet it is this very central aspect of Christianity which
attracts the committed Christian and makes it impossible for him
to accept the otherwise persuasive arguments that Christianity
is a redundancy in the modern world. How can Christianity
be redundant in a world which needs love so much? If we call
an average citizen John Smith, then John Smith has enough of
politicians who think of him as a vote, of civil servants who
think of him as a case under section 53 sub-section C of the Act,
of doctors who think of him as a straightforward appendix, or,
for that matter, of ministers of religion who think of him as a
pastoral visit in district 16. No doubt all these people are doing a
very useful job. But John Smith also needs those who will think
of him as John Smith, who will give him that understanding
which is integral to love. He needs Christians.

Or, to put the matter the other way round, how can any
Christian who has begun, however falteringly, to live the life
of love, turn back? Even to have started to try and love those
whom one finds difficult and uncongenial is to realise that one is
committed to the most fascinating and rewarding of all ad-
ventures, an adventure which will contain many setbacks and
will assuredly not leave one unchanged, but which is something
quite *sui generis*.

But the religion of the Bible, besides inculcating love, in-
culcates truth in the inward parts. And the Christian who
tries to face up to the latter demand is forced to admit that
there is, if not an inherent flaw, at least a deeply rooted
contradiction in his religion. Christians may be committed to a
life of love, but often enough they have behaved quite execrably
toward one another. We have seen that their lovelessness goes
right back to the beginnings of Christianity and it runs right
through its course. Over against the noble trio of saint, martyr

and missionary stands the ignoble one of heresy hunter, inquisitor and torturer. Even if for the moment we leave aside the
ecclesiastics, those manipulators of power, we can see how lovelessness infects the theologians in varying degrees. There is
Tertullian with his facility for saying unkind things in a memor-
able way, Augustine with his preposterous depreciation of
marriage as licensed fornication, a view not unconnected with
his own abandonment of the woman who has been his mistress,
Luther with his betrayal of the Peasants to name only a few.
There is the carnage of the religious wars. Even in our own
secular age Christians can still give one another hell. If there is
anyone who has never seen one fellow Christian give another
a nervous breakdown or never been present at a meeting of
ecclesiastical top brass where the atmosphere could most aptly be
described as coronary creating, then he is more fortunate than
the present writer.

Ibsen has said that there is no word more full of lies and traps
than the little word 'love'. It is only too obvious that at times
the Christians have told some of the lies and fallen into some of
the traps. Sensitive people have found the consequent lovelessness very trying. I have read somewhere that Simon Weil was
kept from becoming a Christian by the two words, 'anathema
sit'—'let him be accursed'. These words which were subsequently used to denounce heretics, make their first appearance
in Christian literature in the letters of St. Paul. That fact in itself ought to warn us of the deep rooted nature of what I have
called the flaw or contradiction in Christian living. St. Paul, the
man who used these words of a fellow Christian, admittedly of
an hypothetical and loveless one, is the man who wrote the
magnificent hymn to love in the very same letter. If the contradiction is found in him, it is likely to be embedded fairly
deeply in each of us, and we are not likely to get rid of it simply
by being carried away by the Ecumenical Movement.

So much will be found in this book by way of criticism of the
politics of the Ecumenical Movement that it would be quite improper to begin without a sincere tribute to the spirit behind the
Movement. It is based on a sensitive appreciation that unloving Christians are a contradiction in terms and in conception

it is a genuine attempt to overcome that contradiction. Nothing in this book is intended to deprive the Ecumenical Movement of this credit and it is a very large credit item indeed. Nor is there any attempt to deny the contribution made by the Ecumenical Movement in producing what in the next chapter is called the Thaw. Any criticism of the Ecumenical Movement in this book is to the effect that its projected solution of the contradiction of Christian lovelessness by means of a series of ecclesiastical mergers is so grotesquely superficial that in the end it can only exacerbate the problem, and has indeed already begun to do so. This is because the Ecumenical Movement refuses to face up to the fact of power. In the *Observer* of 1st January 1967 there is a very moving article by Dr. Charles Davis entitled, 'Why I left the Roman Catholic Church'. In the course of it he writes, 'As for papal documents, I sometimes think there is need for a new science of Vaticanology, in order to discover which pressure groups have succeeded in getting their way and to interpret in the light of the current Roman background the more cryptic references to opinions vaguely reprobated.' Only those with first-hand knowledge of Catholic ecclesiastical politics could meet the need indicated by Dr. Davis and produce his new science of Vaticanology. And this book, apart from the present introductory sector, was written before Dr. Davis' article was published. But I wonder if, *mutatis mutandis*, his sentence does not describe what I have tried, however inexpertly to do in connexion with a field of ecclesiastical politics familiar to me, the relations between my own church, the Church of Scotland, and the Church of England. This is, in Dr. Davis' language, a contribution to a Scoto-Lambethology. Perhaps, however, the most important thing about the ecclesiastical corridors of power is not where they are located, but whether the activity that goes on in them coheres with the demand for love and truth in the inward parts, which is basic to the ecclesiastic's religion. For that reason the story told here may be of interest to those otherwise not concerned with the church affairs of a remote northern land.

At this stage a few words should be added, for the sake of the general reader, to describe what the Ecumenical Movement actually is. It owes its origin to the Edinburgh Missionary Conference of 1910. At this gathering of 1,355 delegates there were representatives not only of the Protestant missionary societies, but also of Anglo-Catholic ones. It was the latter who were quick to see the new possibilities for activity in the field of ecclesiastical politics and to develop the situation. Only four months after the Edinburgh Conference, the Anglican communion in the United States, the Protestant Episcopal Church passed a resolution in its House of Deputies and House of Bishops which ran as follows, 'That a joint commission be appointed to bring about a Conference for the consideration of questions touching Faith and Order, and that all Christian Communions throughout the world which confess our Lord Jesus Christ as God and Saviour be asked to unite with us in arranging for and conducting such a Conference.' The American Anglicans had their setbacks in bringing about such a conference. There was the First World War for one thing. And there were what Mr. John Lawrence, the Anglican who gives a readable account of the history of the Movement,[1] calls 'misconceptions'. Apparently there were those who were foolish enough to imagine that the Anglicans were actually going to make some concessions and there were those among the German churches who knew a piece of Anglican empire building when they saw it. But the American Anglicans went doggedly on. In 1920 they were able to call a meeting in Geneva of the representatives of about seventy churches to decide 'what subjects should be prepared for the World Conference'. The Conference, when it finally took place at Lausanne, was by all accounts something of a shambles.[2] But it passed a Call to Unity. The first sentence of this runs as follows, 'God wills unity. Our presence in this Conference bears testimony to our desire to bend our wills to His. However we may justify the beginnings of disunion, we lament its continuance and henceforth must labour, in penitence and faith, to build up our broken walls.'[3]

---

1. In *The Hard Facts of Unity* (S. C. M.).
2. There were at it 'great differences' according to the article in *The Oxford Dictionary of the Christian Church* on 'Lausanne'.
3. Bell, *Documents on Christian Unity* 1st & 2nd Series Oxford, p.159.

The Conference also passed a section on the Ministry of the Church of which the following passage is an extract. 'In view of (1) the place which the Episcopate, the Councils of Presbyters, and the Congregation of the faithful, respectively, had in the constitution of the early Church, and (2) the fact that episcopal, presbyteral, and congregational systems of government are each to-day, and have been for centuries, accepted by great communions in Christendom and (3) the fact that episcopal, presbyteral, and congregational systems are each believed by many to be essential to the good order of the Church, we therefore recognize that these several elements must all, under conditions which require further study, have an appropriate place in the order of life of a reunited Church, and that each separate communion, recalling the abundant blessing of God vouchsafed to its ministry in the past, should gladly bring to the common life of the united Church its own spiritual treasures.'

These two passages from the Lausanne Declaration form a fascinating introduction to the language of the Ecumenical Movement and the double-think and double-talk it inevitably entails. In the first passage the delegates to the Conference ascribe their presence there to a desire to bend their wills to the will of God. But if anything brought them there, it was the dogged and determined will of the American Anglican Church.[1] But there is no mention of this in the Declaration which coyly attributes the occurrence of the Conference to the agency of the Almighty. This apparently excessive modesty on the part of the American Protestant Episcopal Church paid off for it enabled the aims of that church in bringing about the Conference to be quietly identified with the divine purpose. The services of the Deity thus called in to underwrite the recent diplomatic activity of the American Anglican body are further enlisted to carry out an extensive programme of church liquidation. God, the Lausanne Declaration informs us (quite without proof) wills unity. That is to say all the churches except one are to be

1. 'Christendom's debt to the Protestant Episcopal Church in the early stages of the Faith and Order Movement is beyond calculation. The idea of the Faith and Order Conference, the promotion of the idea on a world scale, and the money that made it possible, all came from that church.' J. Lawrence, *The Hard Facts of Unity*, p.31.

exterminated. Which is to remain and which are to disappear is made clear by the second extract we have cited. This is the famous Lausanne statement which is still regarded in ecumenical circles as the authoritative blueprint for negotiations between uniting churches. It is a quite masterly expression of the basic principle of ecumenical language. It draws the picture, that is to say, of a course of action quite different from the one which it actually proposes. It draws a touching picture of all the different churches, each of them making its own worthwhile contribution to the church of the future. This reunited church is to contain episcopal, presbyteral and congregational elements. This apparently equitable judgment is, in fact, a travesty of equity. Any episcopal church need only make some minor adjustment giving some sort of place to the voice of the non-episcopal clergy and laymen in order to claim that it contains within itself presbyteral and congregational elements. No non-episcopal church, on the other hand, can possibly claim to contain within itself the elements of episcopal government. The famous Lausanne Declaration is the death warrant of all non-episcopal churches. It is the charter of Anglican imperialism. As long as it is regarded as authoritative, in any negotiations between an Anglican and a Protestant church the latter will have to make all the real concessions and the former only trivial ones.

One must pay tribute to the American Protestant Episcopal Church for the seventeen years of intense political activity which led to its triumph at Lausanne. It was, in fact, one of the most daring pieces of ecclesiastical imperialism ever carried out. While their Church of England brethren were basking in the delusive twilight of the last years of English power, the American Anglicans had no illusions about their weakness as an ecclesiastical power group in the United States. Less than 2 per cent of the population of that country, they knew they could not hope to rival numerically the much stronger non-episcopal Protestant communions in America. By using the financial resources in which lay perhaps their greatest strength, by unwearying and skilful ecclesiastical diplomacy, they secured in a distant Swiss town the settlement that could well result in the extinction of these other churches and the absorption of their personnel and resources into the Anglican system.

No one, of course, saw it like that, any more than Chamberlain saw Munich as a surrender. For this opaqueness of ecumenical action, ecumenical language is, as we have seen, in no small measure responsible. Its function seems always to have been to provide a vehicle whereby imperialist action can be denied quite honestly by those who are carrying it out or conniving at it. For the rest it must be remembered that the pre- and post-Lausanne activity of the Ecumenical Movement has taken place within the context of the situation outlined at the beginning of this chapter. There is an increasing sensitivity to the fact that loveless Christianity is a contradiction in terms and increasing effort to overcome lovelessness between Christians of different denominations. This situation while highly laudable in itself and productive of much real good in the ecumenical simply plays into the hand of the ecclesiastical power operator. If only he can disguise his imperialism as love—and ecumenical language enables him to do just that even from himself—his critic can easily be made to appear, even in his own eyes, as one who sins against love. The critic's guilt complex can be further enlarged by the ecclesiastical power operator's lack of reluctance—evident as early as Lausanne—to identify his own actions with those of God. The present inter-church situation is therefore a very confused one, which could well lead to tragedy unless some effort is made to distinguish the unity sought by love from that sought by power. An attempt will be made in the next chapter to distinguish some of the more obvious features of the present situation.

2

The Present Situation

THE most important development of the Ecumenical Movement since the Second World War has been the formation at Amsterdam in 1948 of the World Council of Churches. The continuity of this body with the movement set afoot by the American Anglicans so many years before is seen in the fact that—in spite of a trenchant criticism by Professor Bultmann[1]— it defines the Basis of its Constitution in terms of the motion passed in the House of Deputies and House of Bishops of the Protestant Episcopal Church.[2] 'The World Council of Churches is a fellowship of churches which accept our Lord Jesus Christ as God and Saviour.' The authority of the World Council lies in an Assembly which meets every five years.[3] Seats in this Assembly are given to official representatives of the member churches, that is to say they are hardly likely to come the way of those who are not in favour with the establishments of their respective churches. The allocation of seats to the various churches admits of readjustment and this is obviously a field which leaves room for a good deal of activity in the sphere of ecclesiastical politics as does the securing of seats on the Praesidium and the Central Committee which meets annually and appoints its own Executive. But the World Council recognises the limitation of its powers. It does not legislate for the individual churches. According to a report received by its Central Committee in 1950

1. In *Essays* tr. by J. C. G. Greig, S. C. M., p. 273.
2. Cf. p.
3. The Constitution of the World Council of Churches will be found in Bell, Documents on Christian Unity 4th Series p. 201.

it is not a Super-Church. It does not negotiate unions between churches, which the latter must carry out on their own initiative.

Within its limits, which are obviously greater than those of the Vatican, the World Council of Churches is an ecclesiastical power concentration. It maintains a sizeable bureaucracy. It would be strange if it were not in the ecclesiastical sense of the word, a hive of political activity. Many of the functions of the World Council of Churches are entirely laudable. By facilitating common action by the churches and promoting co-operation in study, it has fostered ends which are good in themselves and which have played their part in what we shall go on to describe as the Thaw. In these respects the World Council has obviously done something to remove the contradiction of loveless Christianity. Has it done anything to strengthen and perpetuate that contradiction?

It has done this in two connected ways. By speaking of disunity, e.g. in its Evanston Report, as disobedience and sin, it has committed itself to a ruthless and inveterate attack on denominations. It has quite failed to see that Denominationalism, just as much as all that is good in the Ecumenical Movement, arose as an honest attempt to deal with the painful contradiction that antipathies flourish within the religion of love (a contradiction which had existed for centuries before the rise of denominations). Denominationalism, the courageous abandonment of the nightmare dogma of the One Church, was an attempt to overcome that basic flaw in Christianity as it had manifested itself in the horrors of the religious wars. It is the conviction that if you cannot agree with your fellow Christians, it is better to live with than to kill them. Denominationalism is a valuable device which enables you honestly and openly to disagree with your fellow Christians on what for them are fundamentals and what for you are over-beliefs and vice versa. It enables you to do this and yet not deprive them, or be deprived by them, of the ordinances of the Christian religion. It is this basically far from ignoble attempt to overcome the contradiction of lovelessness apparently inherent in Christianity that the World Council seems incapable of separating from the perversions which it has suffered, very often at the hands of those who have covertly clung to the dogma of the One Church. Meant as a device whereby Christians could be less unloving to each other, Denominationalism has been turned into a pretext for lovelessness, for adding fuel to the hostility of rival racial groups or rival football teams and for that Schadenfreude masquerading as thought which has led Christians to deny the name of 'church' to the assemblies of their fellow Christians. This goes to show that Denominationalism has not been completely successful in eradicating lovelessness from Christians. But the World Council is not going to either and the Ecumenicals who think that it is are rather like those optimists who think they can get the dent out of a burst ball. Nothing is more amusing than to hear an Ecumenical enthusiast thank God very rightly for the fact that he no longer harbours acrimonious feelings toward Catholics or Protestants without realising that he now feels that way about those in his own communion who cannot conscientiously become Anglicans.

In singling out Denominationalism for attack, the World Council has too easily assumed that a desire for unity and love are the same thing. It obviously cannot cure the contradiction of lovelessness in Christians for this took place within the One Church and long before there were denominations, e.g. the treatment of Abelard and the suppression of the Albigensians. In all this, of course, it had been quite unfair to denominations. Instead of curing the patient it has devoted its energies to denouncing his previous medical adviser.

The other way in which the World Council has strengthened and perpetuated the lovelessness in Christianity is that by uncritically extolling unity it has advanced the imperialist aspirations of ecclesiastical power concentrations. The documents of the World Council are singularly reticent about such factors as ecclesiastical politics and ecclesiastical power. This is not surprising for the delegates to its Assemblies are *personae gratae* to the establishments of the constituent churches, that is, to those who through successful political activity hold the power in these churches. Ecclesiastical politicians are notoriously cagey about their activities. They tend, when successful, to ascribe them to God. We have seen how, when as the Anglican

Ecumenical John Lawrence agrees, seventeen years of dogged and expensive diplomatic work on the part of the American Protestant Episcopal Church brought about the Lausanne Conference, the delegates blandly said, 'Our presence in this Conference bears testimony to our desire to bend our wills to His.' As we shall see later in this book, the ascription of his own successful activities to God is an age-old device of the ecclesiastical power operator. It makes it so embarrassing for anyone else to try and undo what he has done. It is not surprising therefore if in the utterances of the World Council there is very little about the political activity that goes on within it and a great deal about what God has done or what God wills.

One wonders how far the ecclesiastical politician blinds himself to the naked realities of power and it is hard to say whether some of the pronouncements of the World Council on church union are disingenuous or simply naive. Take this statement from the Evanston Report[1] 'By planting the Cross of Christ in the midst of our divisions we believe He will overrule all their sin and make them serve His purpose of unity. Concretely, this means that when churches, in their actual historical situations, reach a point of readiness and a time of decision, then their witnessing may require obedience unto death. They may then have to be prepared to offer up some of their accustomed inherited forms of life in uniting with other churches without complete certainty as to all that will emerge from the step of faith.' Can one really imagine a Pope giving up some of the accustomed, inherited forms of the life of his church in order to unite with the Waldensians? Or can one imagine an Archbishop of Canterbury saying to his advisers, 'O.K. boys, this is the time of decision when we are going to make the step of faith and be obedient unto death. Let us ring down the curtains on the Church of England and unite with the Baptists!'? Top Christians did not converge on Evanston from all over the world to suggest anything so ludicrous. Their utterance which we have quoted above is simply an exhortation to ecclesiastical flies to walk into the webs of ecclesiastical spiders. The Cross of Christ, on the other hand is the laying down by the Son of God

1. Bell, Documents on Christian Unity, 4th Series, p. 237.

of his power in order to die the death of a criminal. To mention it in connexion with an appeal for ecclesiastical take-over bids is both inappropriate and lacking in good taste.

Until the World Council talks with a little less glib facility about God's Will and with a little more frankness about the facts of politics and the realities of power within itself and all great ecclesiastical concentrations, it will stand under the suspicion of pandering to the lust for power which is only satisfied with that unity we call monopoly.

*　　*　　*

Quite apart from the official meetings of the World Council and its equally official utterances, there is another facet of the present inter-church situation which must be mentioned. This is the quite informal aspect of it that it is now much more easy for Protestant ministers and Catholic priests to get to know one another, to talk frankly and to become friends. This is a quite priceless benefit and if the Ecumenical Movement has had something to do with bringing it about, all honour to it. This is an opening of closed horizons. Its value lies in its informality. For in this type of fellowship there is something that is lacking in a doctor's examination of a patient, a lawyer's cross-examination of a witness or a meeting between two political parties. There is mutual openness, a readiness on the part of each to let his own horizon be changed in the light of what he learns from being afforded this glimpse into that of the other.[1] There is no saying what this could lead to if it were allowed to develop. The trouble is that followers of the Ecumenical Movement are always trying to transform it into its opposite, namely, political talks with a view to securing some ecclesiastical merger. Here again the Ecumenical Movement has got the dent out of one part of the ball only to have it reappear in another. It has made talk between those of different communions easy and informal; it has made talk between those of the same communion difficult because political. It is possible if one is a Church of Scotland minister to have an interesting and valuable conversa-

1. This analysis of the different kinds of talk owes much to H. Gadamer's book *Wahrheir und Methode*, Tübingen.

tion with a Catholic priest on the ordination of women. But it is impossible to have that kind of conversation with the members of the Ecumenical or pro-Anglican party in the Church of Scotland. With them such an issue cannot be discussed on its merits. For they know that the ordination of women is unacceptable to Lambeth and the main plank on the platform of their ecclesiastical party is the reconstitution of the Church of Scotland on lines acceptable to Lambeth. So they know they have to find Biblical passages which oppose the ordination of women. They think they have enough of these and are ready to tell one what they are. One can go on talking to them but one senses they are not really listening. They are no doubt thinking on what for them are more important things—securing the right conveners and the right committee majorities to get their party policy carried through.

*   *   *

Besides the Thaw there is the Ferment. The Ferment is a more complicated affair and the questions which have given rise to it can only be mentioned here and not discussed in detail, still less answered. The Ferment is observable in such phenomena as Demythologizing, the Bishop of Woolwich, the American Death of God theologians, the new morality and the new theology and Dr. Davis' departure from the Catholic Church. What is the hidden yeast that has caused the ferment? It has nothing to do with the Ecumenical Movement save to the slight degree in which it has facilitated the transmission of ideas to churches where the theologian is weak *vis-à-vis* the ecclesiastic from churches where he is reasonably independent. We have seen that the World Council Assembly is composed of those acceptable to the establishments of the various churches. Establishments do not like ferments. This has been an age extraordinarily rich in really great theologians, men like Barth, Bultmann and Tillich. It is significant that none of them has taken much part in the assemblies of the World Council. They play in a different league.

Again, I do not think it wise to say that the yeast which has produced the Ferment is an un-Christian one. One of the most

melancholy ecclesiastical occasions of recent years occurred in
the General Assembly of the Church of Scotland when the
Moderator of that body congratulated the Archbishop of Canterbury for having rebuked the Bishop of Woolwich for producing the book, *Honest to God*. In that book the three main
sources of the Bishop's thought are Tillich, Bultmann and Bonhoeffer. Of these three, Tillich, because of his Christianity, at
a fairly advanced age, suffered exile to a country of whose
language he was ignorant, Bultmann, because of his Christianity, said one or two rather dangerous things at a time when
his country was under the Nazi régime, Bonhoeffer died for his
faith. It is mercifully a long time since a Scots Moderator or an
English Archbishop had to suffer, run risks or die for his faith.
But men are hardly likely to do these things unless they believe
in Christianity. It was perhaps unwise for the one ecclesiastic to
congratulate the other on his rebuke to one who had drawn his
inspiration from sources so well tested.

To say that is not to justify everything that has been said or
done as part of the Ferment. The present writer is not competent and this is not the place to attempt an objective judgment on
the question whether the Death of God theologians should still
be in their communion or whether Dr. Davis should have left
his. All that can be done here is to indicate some of the causes of
the Ferment. One of these is undoubtedly the rise of critical
history as an academic study. One might argue, for instance,
that the tension in Bultmann arises from the fact that as an
evangelist he is concerned to proclaim the action of God and as
a critical historian he is precluded from finding God as a causal
agent when he studies the documents of the New Testament.
There is the curious connexion between Christianity and
secularism established by such thinkers as Gogarten and Von
Weizäcker and based on the fact that Christianity undoubtedly
helped to rid the world of demons, the gods which are no gods of St.
Paul. Whether that really enables us to reach the reconciliation
between Christianity and the Logical Analysts who contend
that the conception of God is a meaningless one which Van
Buren advocates may well be doubted. But it is not for Ecumenicals who have done so much to reduce the concept of God

to a device in ecclesiastical politics to object if the dominant English trend in post war philosophy has difficulty with the concept of God. Then there is the dominant school of post-war continental philosophy, existentialism, stressing existence rather than essence and so making it difficult to understand the God-man's union of two natures as this is formulated in the classical creeds of Nicaea and Chalcedon.

Last, and by no means least there are the changing attitudes to sex. Here the change in ̣our patterns has been bewilderingly rapid and complex, and any brief comment is patently inadequate. But perhaps it can be said that in this field the ferment is in part due to the difficulty of applying the traditional Christian standards, drawn up in an era of male dominance in an age where the status of woman has become very different.

There is no doubt that the Ferment is quite a ferment. There are those in the churches who would couple it with broken speed limits, city gangs, gaols with easy exits, teachers afraid of their pupils and casual sexual relationships as simply another aspect of the glissade of the nineteen-sixties towards anarchy. For those who see the Ferment that way, the remedy for it is increased ecclesiastical authority. The trouble is that the Ferment is challenging ecclesiastical authority in the name of truth. What really goes on at a Vatican Council or in official negotiations between churches under the influence of the Ecumenical Movement? How far is it really something authoritative and therefore binding on men's consciences? How far is it simply a struggle in ecclesiastical politics in which the winning side quite unscrupulously and blasphemously identifies its activities with the will and action of God? Until that question has been honestly faced there can be no real restoration of ecclesiastical authority. The present book is an attempt to provide a partial answer to it by an account of events in the only ecclesiastical area of which the writer has first-hand knowledge.

The confrontation between the Church of Scotland and the Church of England is interesting because it is an example of what happens when a church better able to contain the Ferment

meets a church more favoured in the power struggle of ecclesiastical take over bids which is canonized by the Ecumenical
Movement as the Will of God. Church of England bishops can
still discipline the innocent divorced who remarry, whereas as
far back as the seventeenth century the Church of Scotland was
criticizing the Pope[1] for his cruelty to that very class of people.
In the intellectual sphere it is hard to envisage the Church of
England agreeing to the setting up of a One Church which did
not enforce subscription to the classic creeds of Nicaea and
Chalcedon. The Church of Scotland minister, on the other
hand, enjoys a high degree of intellectual freedom, being required to subscribe to the fundamental doctrines of the Christian
faith as contained in the Westminster Confession, but being
allowed to decide for himself what these fundamental doctrines
are. It would seem that the Church of Scotland is less rigid and
so more able to contain the Ferment along with other and
more conservative expressions of Christianity.

In the field of ecclesiastical diplomacy, where the Ecumenical
Movement's influence has meant that negotiations are carried
on according to the rules of that great charter of Anglican imperialism, the Lausanne Declaration, the boot is very much on
the other foot. The propaganda of the Ecumenical Movement
has brought about within the Church of Scotland a minority
but formidable group of Anglican fellow travellers whose political skill has enabled them to gain control of such vital committees as the Inter-Church Relations Committee and the Panel on
Doctrine. This Anglican or Ecumenical party has also been
able to secure a majority on all the important negotiating committees with other churches. At least this took place until very
recently. In November 1966, after criticism of the unrepresenta-
tive character of the latest of these committees, the Commission
of the General Assembly requested the nominating body to re-
vise the list of members. In the circumstances, it is not surprising that the Church of Scotland is fighting a desperate
battle to save itself from being reconstituted under a handful of
Anglican consecrated bishops, who, if ever they were asked to the
Lambeth Conference, would form a very small minority there.

1. In the National Covenant.

But we are not concerned here with the details of the Anglo-Scottish ecclesiastical confrontation but only to note that they conform to a pattern. It is hard to see how this pattern can be avoided when a church which has accepted the message of the Aufklärung confronts one like the Catholic Church, which has rejected it, or one like the Anglican Church whose greatest modern infusion of strength has been when it was enlivened by the Oxford Movement, one of the finest products of Romanticism, the great rival of the Aufklärung. To put it bluntly, in the former type of church the power ratio between the theologian and the ecclesiastic is in favour of the first, in the latter it is in favour of the second. The former church will be able to contain the Ferment, the latter will win the struggle in ecclesiastical diplomacy which the Ecumenical Movement has both proclaimed as a holy war and fitted out with a set of crooked rules. That is the dilemma of contemporary Christianity.

The power equations make it easy to see where the alternatives lie. The freezing of ecclesiastical diplomacy on the lines laid down by the Lausanne Declaration mean the extinction of Protestantism and the creation of a vast Anglican empire. The confrontation of this with the Roman Catholic Church would then presumably result in an ecclesiastical structure to the right of Anglicanism and the left of Rome as we know them today. Then what the Ecumenical Movement sincerely, but surely quite blasphemously, calls the Will of God will come about. This is the creation of a monopoly power structure where the individual believer who disagreed, however conscientiously, with the holders of ecclesiastical power would, if he persisted, be denied the ordinances of the Christian religion. In such a monopoly structure of power is there any guarantee that the ordinary believer would not have to submit his conscience to the views of those adroit in ecclesiastical politics? Is there any guarantee that there would be any place in it, not just for the wilder spirits of the Ferment, but for men like Tillich and Bultmann, concerned to reach an expression of Christianity comparable with the new learning and social conditions, whom we have seen to be ready to suffer or hazard for the Christian faith, but neither of whom could honestly sign the Nicaean or Chalcedonian creeds? If the loss of this type of Christian is the price of unity, it is too great an offence against love and truth to deprive him of the Word and Sacraments. One must surely hope for the other alternative, that a world which knows that there is so much worse wrong with it than the fact that American Congregationalists and Presbyterians have different head offices, will become bored with the World Council's tirades against disunity.

PART TWO

The Concept of Oneness

3

Which Oneness?

'T HAT they may all be one.' These words are an injunction of our Lord. There is therefore the more need to ask soberly what kind of oneness they enjoin. For there are at least three kinds of oneness. Consider the following three statements:

'Two souls with but a single thought. Two hearts that beat as one.'

'Oxford and Cambridge are virtually the one way into the Foreign Service.'

'One Volk, one Reich, one Führer.'

In the first of these statements oneness is an expression of love. Oneness may be a synonym for love, though I do not think it ever brings out the full depth of the latter term. We do not love properly unless we respect the otherness of the other person whom we love. It is not without significance that Christian theology, in stressing that love has its home in God, has found it necessary to think of Him, not as one, but as triune.

In the second of these statements oneness expresses a claim to exclusiveness. Here, oneness does not join (as it does when it is a synonym for love) but severs. Certain entities (in this case two universities) possess something (in this case entry to the Foreign Service) which no other entities of the same kind possess.

In the third of these statements oneness expresses a will to power. In this particular case it expresses Hitler's will to power. If a will to power is so strong that it can tolerate no rival then it will naturally express itself in a demand for oneness.

I do not think that the prayer of the Johannine Christ, 'that they may be one' lays any obligation on us to seek a oneness which gives expression to a claim to exclusiveness or a will to power. For the incarnation, a central doctrine of Christianity, tells how the Son of God laid aside his heavenly power to live the life of a man. And the earthly Jesus spent not a little of his time withstanding the claim of the Pharisees to exclusiveness. Further, most Christians today do not find it easy to defend either exclusiveness or an imperialistic will to power in non-ecclesiastical matters.

On the other hand Jesus Christ is the revelation of the love of God. Christians are therefore clearly enjoined to seek oneness in so far as it is an expression of love. When the Johannine Christ prays that we may all be one, he is laying on us the injunction to love one another. This is a very difficult injunction indeed, for it is far from easy to love people whom we find uncongenial and trying. But this is the heart of Christianity and there is no evading it if we want to be Christians. In calling on their young officer cadets to promise to love the unlovable, the Salvation Army authorities are summoning them to undertake at once the burden and the adventure of Christian living.

We have perhaps come far enough to make two initial criticisms of the Ecumenical Movement. In the ecclesiastical sphere the adherents of the Movement engage in intense political activity and incessant propaganda to bring about oneness. It never occurs to them to analyse the term 'oneness' and to look at the more discreditable as well as the more creditable drives which lie behind any movement toward oneness. Once this were done it would certainly be more difficult to describe, as is frequently done, the whole movement as an activity of the Holy Spirit (with the convenient implication that anyone critical of it is opposing the Holy Spirit). But it would be conducive to clarity. Ecumenicals have never had many inhibitions in querying the motives of their opponents. C. H. Dodd's work on non-theological obstacles to union has had a lot of success. Is it too much to ask them to search their own?

The other point is to ask how far the work carried on by and the goal envisaged by the Ecumenical Movement has helped Christians to carry out their Lord's command to love one another. On the credit side, and it is a very big item, goes the improvement in relations between Catholics and Protestants which the Ecumenical Movement has helped to bring about. Protestants have a clear obligation to love Catholics. No one in their senses can fail to be thankful that the dreadful relation of hostility and suspicion which far too often prevailed between Catholic and Protestant has so largely disappeared.

But real and thankful appreciation of this cannot blind us to the limitations of the Ecumenical ideas of oneness. Putting all Christians within the one denomination will not cure the sin of lovelessness for the obvious reason that the worst examples of lovelessness do not occur between but within denominations. The Fenelon-Bousset controversy, the acrimonious Bishops' Debate in the church of Scotland are striking examples of how within the one denomination men can drive love, and with love, Christ, out of their relations with one another. But every parish squabble and every presbytery or diocesan vendetta is an equal offence against love which no amount of ecclesiastical mergers can cure. Today indeed it is much easier for a Protestant minister to love Catholics than to love his own office bearers. It is the latter, not the former, whom he has to live with and who touch his complexes and neuroses at their most sensitive point.

We shall have something to say later on the oft-repeated Ecumenical prayer for forgiveness for the sin of disunity. All that need be said here is that to pray for forgiveness for denominational differences held honestly and with mutual respect, and to say nothing about the bitter rancours that we all know can find a lodging within the most ecumenically minded theological college staffs, cathedral chapters and congregational boards is to become guilty of something like frivolity.

4

Can the Church Sin?

I n the last chapter we tried to analyse oneness with a view to
finding what human drives and claims find their attainment in
something that can be called oneness. The conclusion was that
oneness is indeed an ambiguous term, that human urges both
laudable and highly reprehensible can find fulfilment in a state
of affairs not inaptly described as oneness. The implication
would seem to be that whenever oneness is set up as an ideal,
it cannot simply be taken at its face value, but must be examined with a view to finding who is seeking what in this particular case of oneness. Only then are we in a position to say
whether this particular instance of oneness is the good thing it is
made out to be.

Let us now leave analysis for a more empirical approach.
When we come across oneness in life do we, in fact, welcome it
as a good thing? Sometimes we do as when after a great deal
of argument a meeting reaches a common mind. It is true that
after the meeting we may wonder if the oneness may not be
more apparent than real and be the result of skilled chairman-
ship or sheer weariness rather than a real coming together of
minds. And if we are wise we will recognise that that kind of
oneness is impossible on issues where people are doctrinally
divided or where they are determined to play party politics
against one another. Nevertheless, on occasions where we
achieve this kind of oneness we welcome it.

Oneness, however, is not always welcomed as a good thing.
Thus when Sticko Glue and Clingo Adhesive Paste join forces
to become the one glue producers in their country, their fellow

citizens do not generally go into raptures about this triumph of ecumenicity and the rise of the one glue company. So far from attributing this achievement of unity to the Holy Spirit, the ordinary citizen will rather be inclined to see behind it such factors as financial imperialism and the techniques of the take-over bid. Public disapproval of the one glue company may indeed go further and invoke trust-busting or anti-monopolistic practices legislation. Here is a case where oneness means monopoly and monopoly means an unhealthy concentration of power.

Does this hold where the monopoly is an ecclesiastical one? Does the one church involve an unhealthy concentration of power? I think some effort should be made to give an empirical answer to this question. After all, there are parts of the world like Spain, Cyprus and Malta where there is virtually one church. Is it the view of those who have experience of such a state of affairs that it is, in fact, a good one? In a country with one church is there any future for those, who, however conscientiously, for any reason oppose the hierarchy? Is dissent, however honestly expressed, not inevitably driven outside the church and thus deprived of the ordinances of the Christian religion? To put the matter bluntly, are men freed from the temptations of monopolistic power simply because they fasten their collars at the back?

I think that questions like these should be answered empirically and I suspect that answers given on the basis of experience would be disquieting to supporters of the Ecumenical Movement. It must be pointed out, however, that in certain denominations the view prevails that the church is so different from a merely human institution like a glue company that it is absurd to carry out empirical tests to find whether the ecclesiastical authorities of the one succumb to the temptations of the directors of the latter. On this view the church is the continuation of the Incarnation and where it is properly constituted it cannot err. Is not the Pope the vicar of Christ, or at any rate, are not the bishops the successors of the apostles?

The first thing we must say about this view is that it is held by many sincere and deeply committed Christians. The second is that this question, can the Church properly constituted and acting *qua* church, sin and reject Christ? has been curiously neglected by the Ecumenical movement. Yet it is a vital one. The view that the church is divinely safeguarded from sin means a very great deal to those who hold it. I cannot imagine them wishing to be in the same denomination with those who like myself (for reasons I shall state below) reject it. But if neither of us, as I trust, wishes to deprive the other of the ordinances of the Christian religion, that means at least two denominations.

Let me now outline my reason for taking one side on this basic question which has divided and will continue to divide Christians. As long as there are two minds about Rolf Hochhuth's play *Der Stellvertreter* there cannot be one church. For my part I accept Hochhuth's thesis that the real representative of Christ is not the Pope who failed to protest when the S.S. commander in Rome sent the city's Jews to extermination, but the simple priest who took one Jew's place in the extermination train. I recognise that Hochhuth's thesis must be indescribably painful to a Catholic (though, to be blunt, not nearly so painful as extermination was to a Jew). But to be fair to Hochhuth it must be pointed out that he has some precedent in making his thesis. The theme of Dostoevsky's story of the Grand Inquisitor in *The Brothers Karamazov*, is that Jesus Christ is just as likely to be rejected by the Church of the New Testament as he was by the Church of the Old Testament. Similarly, Karl Barth writes in his Gifford Lectures, 'In settling this question about the true church, the decisive factor is not the antiquity of the Church, as the Scottish Confession says (e.g. Cain was older than Abel) nor is it the place (Jerusalem was the city of God and Christ was crucified in it), nor is it succession (for such succession was to be found in the family of Aaron, which contained ultimately an Annas and a Caiaphas) nor are numbers decisive (The Scribes and Pharisees were more numerous than the disciples of Jesus).'[1] Barth is maintaining that the Church of the New Testament has no more than the Church of the Old Testament, any safeguards which will guarantee it against a possible rejection of Jesus Christ.

1. *The Knowledge of God and the Service of God*, p. 170.

So much for a citation of authors who have been concerned to point out that it is possible for the official church, however constituted, to reject Christ. Nor is it easy to see how the church which is always a power structure can be a continuation of the incarnation which is God's renunciation of power. Also, and here we touch on a theme which will be developed throughout this book, it seems not a little likely that the view that the church when properly constituted, cannot reject Christ, is itself an expression of ecclesiastical imperialism rather than a theological statement. Any prudent will to power will pay heed to its propaganda department (and may indeed genuinely believe its statements). The ecclesiastical authorities who were responsible for the coining of the word 'propaganda' are hardly likely to be an exception to this. Quite the best way of getting what you want is to persuade other people that it is what God wants. A church that cannot reject Christ is only too obviously a blank cheque for ecclesiastical top brass. No doubt ecclesiastics believe quite genuinely in such a view of the church. After all, Charles I probably quite genuinely believed in the Divine Right of Kings. But then it was very convenient for him to have other people believe it. So much so that it is not easy to credit Charles' particular interpretation of Romans 13 just to straight exegesis.

It might, of course, be argued that the one church has advantages which outweigh the dangers of an ecclesiastical monopoly. It is sometimes said that people are kept from going to church because there are many churches and not one. Here again sober empirical study might show that ecumenical propaganda bears little relation to the truth. After all Sweden, where there is virtually only one church has an extraordinarily low record of church attendance, whereas in the United States, where there is an amazing variety of churches, there is an equally amazingly high record of church attendance.

5

The Ultimate Possibilities

WE have looked at the one church in the light of an analysis of what the term 'oneness' expresses. Then we have tried to see how the one church looks in these situations where it actually exists. Let us now see how the one church appears when we ask what part it has had in bringing about the ultimate possibilities of human existence today.

Human life today is overshadowed by two ultimate possibilities which have risen for the first time in our lifetime. The first is the possibility that all human life will be destroyed by nuclear weapons. The second is the possibility that by the use of torture, mind-conditioning and brain-washing, a race of men will be produced who are not really human at all. Of these possibilities certain things fail to be said. First they are ultimate possibilities, in that either of them, if realised, would cancel out the other possibilities which lie open to the human race. Second, they are possibilities, not actualities, perhaps even possible possibilities rather than actual possibilities. A physicist of the calibre of Professor C. E. von Weizsäcker doubts whether man has as yet the capacity completely to destroy himself and there is no ground for maintaining that a state like that portrayed in Orwell's *1984* has, as yet, ever existed. But the power of evil has been revealed to our century in the horrors of Nazism and it is little comfort to know that there still remains an ever vanishing limit to the techniques of destructions of the race on the one hand and the human spirit on the other.

The two ultimate possibilities can be expressed in theological terms. The destruction of the human race by nuclear weapons would be man's rejection of the Creation. The production, by the techniques of mind conditioning of a race who are not really human any longer would be man's rejection of the Image of God. When seen in these terms the ultimate possibilities are seen to be comparable with the Crucifixion, which was man's rejection of the Incarnation. This analogy with the Crucifixion means that the ultimate possibilities bring with them for the Christian both a message of hope and a summons to repentance. They bring a message of hope, for just as God had an answer to the Crucifixion in the Resurrection, so may God be presumed to have an answer to the ultimate possibilities of our day. The last word on the human race and the human spirit lies not with them but with Him.

But the analogy with the Crucifixion is also a sufficient reminder that the ultimate possibilities summon the Christian Church to heart-searching and repentance. At every Good Friday the Church is called soberly to reflect whether the things that drove Christ to the Cross are still within her and to recognise that every time she has driven out love from her midst, she has driven out Christ. In the same way no serious thinking Christian would wish to evade the plain duty of facing up to the measure of responsibility which the Church bears for the two ultimate possibilities which overshadow our day. I would say that for each of these possibilities the Christian Church bears its share of responsibility and that in each case the idea of the one Church has proved pernicious. Let us see how this is the case.

The discovery of nuclear power has caused a crisis because modern man has become unbalanced. He is rather like a convict in an old-fashioned treadmill some of whose muscles were over-developed and others allowed to atrophy. Intellectually he is developed to the point where he can discover and produce nuclear energy; spiritually he is not developed to the point where he can be trusted not to abuse it. Is the church in any way responsible for this lack of harmony between man's scientific and spiritual development? I think it is. The divorce of scientific development from spiritual and religious factors, the fact, for instance, that members of the Royal Society were forbidden to talk theology can be traced back to man's weariness of the religious wars of the seventeenth century which were fought to secure the one Church. After a century in which biblical exegesis and theology had been prostituted to justify the imperialisms of one version of the one Church after another, it was understandable that men would turn their backs on it. The belief that by getting into the secular atmosphere of a laboratory, man could escape into a world that was clean may have been a dream, finally to be shattered when Einstein and Szilard felt themselves forced to send their letter to the President. It has left us not only with the ultimate appalling possibility of universal human destruction, but with the day-to-day situation in which science and technology are constantly producing social and moral problems which they cannot be expected to solve and which Christianity only belatedly realises to exist. But the dream was a good dream, the dream of decent and able men sickened by the carnage of conflicts like the Thirty Years' War brought about by Christians whose minds were dominated by the idea of the One Church.

For the second possibility, that a state of affairs might be brought about in which men have ceased to be human, the Church is I think even more directly responsible, and again because it has been dominated by the idea of the One Church. Man no longer in the image of God has never been better described than in Orwell's *1984*. In that book, O'Brien, the torturer, in tracing the history of the process, begins with the setting up of the Inquisition by the Christian Church. Where else would he begin? The Romans and their rivals the Phoenicians, were coarse, brutal and savage. No one is going to sentimentalise over them in view of the way they treated prisoners of war, criminals and slaves. But did they deal with men in the way the young Frenchman, e.g. in *The Land of the Great Image* is dealt with at Goa by the Inquisition? When the Christian Church in the interests of the suppression of heresy, i.e. of the establishment of the One Church, set up this institution to condition men's minds by breaking their nerve, it brought a new dimension of evil into existence. The martyrs of the early church made a good confession in the arena. They were able to. The victims of the Christian Church were not. The Holy

Inquisition saw to that. The suppression of the Albigensian heresy does not point back to anything in the ancient world. But it points forward to something like the evidence brought forward during the Eichmann trial.

The conclusions of the last paragraph will not be palatable to many Christians. They are not palatable to the author. But I think they have to be said. They have to be said because Christians like everyone else must face up to themselves. They have also to be said because for years the Ecumenical Movement has been extolling the idea of the One Church without ever facing up to it and because for years it has been telling us Christians to repent of our denominations and never facing up to the possibility that the greatest thing we have to repent of is the idea of the One Church.

6

Power and Exclusiveness

W HAT the origins of the stress laid on the one church are, is something this book does not profess to dogmatize about. It may be that it was highly expedient for the church as for any weak and infant organisation to keep together. When one of the signatories of the Declaration of Independence said, 'Now we must all hang together', Benjamin Franklin, no doubt with the melancholy fate of the Culloden P.O.W.S. before his mind, retorted, 'By God, if we don't, we'll all hang separately'.

The American analogy perhaps holds, for there were times when the Romans were just as ready to crucify the first Christians as the English were to hang the first Americans. The first Christians were indeed much weaker than the first Americans in that for them an appeal to arms was hopeless. All the greater their need for unity.

Or it may be that the notion of the one church is gnostic in origin. This is probably the case if the oneness is connected with the idea that the church is One Body of Christ. The idea that the church is the Body of Christ is extremely useful as a metaphor in preaching. When one is asked, e.g. by the Bishop of Woolwich in his book *The Body*, to treat it not just as a metaphor but as a literal description of the church, then it is very hard to attach any meaning to it. It is very hard to attach any meaning to it as a Christian doctrine, that is to say — it is easy enough to attach a meaning to it if we accept it as a Gnostic infiltration into Christianity. Professor Bultmann's reconstruction of the basic gnostic myth explains it perfectly. According to this myth the demons have captured a heavenly being who has strayed from the realms of glory. The Gnostics, the knowing or spiritual ones, are parts of this heavenly being and when they die, they, fortified by the passwords which have been given to them by a second heavenly being, escape through the realms of the demons to their true heavenly home. A Christianity fitted into this myth will easily enough give the results that Christians are part of the Body of Christ and that, as there is only one body, so there can only be one church. But, if Bultmann's view of Gnosticism is right it will be a Christianity adapted to fit the categories of an alien faith.

The argument of this book does not stand or fall on Bultmann's view of Gnosticism, however attractive that may be. More important than to trace the origin of the stress laid on the one church is to understand its continuing attractiveness for churchmen. Its attractiveness lies in its ambiguity. Churchmen in seeking to establish the one church are encouraged to feel that they are seeking after the oneness of love whereas they, perhaps without any intention of doing so, are working for the oneness of imperialistic will to power or the oneness of exclusiveness. This ambiguity, brought about by the Ecumenical Movement's concentration on propaganda rather than an analysis of its own basic concept has had devastating consequences. We will deal with some of these later. For the present let us try and ask how it is that the will to power and the claim to exclusiveness find a lodging in the hearts of Christians.

Few men have written of the will to power with greater understanding than Reinhold Niebuhr. Basically his view is that the will to power connects with the capacity for self transcendence. To man alone of the animals belongs this ability to stand outside his life and see it for what it is. The vista is a devastating one for human life is pitifully frail and brief. Hence the urge to give it meaning and significance, the urge out of which imperialism grows. It is not without significance that Cecil Rhodes, the arch-imperialist, knew that his life would be even shorter than the normal human span and that Hitler, the would-be founder of a thousand-year Reich should resemble facially the Charlie Chaplin of the silent films, the typical little man of western civilisation. It is understandable too, on Niebuhr's account of the matter, why the temptations of the will to power first become acute in middle age. In our youth when we take ourselves to be immortal we are delivered from the imperialist longings of those who know how brief life is. The temptations of power come to those over the threshold of middle age, not to the glutton, the slothful and the drunkard among them, but to the intelligent and the capable. The novels of C.P. Snow have done much to show the ruthlessness of the struggle for power in academic circles.

C. P. Snow has probably not made himself popular in certain quarters by demythologising the life of a Cambridge college, and certainly anyone who mentions in a gathering of Ecumenicals that there is such a thing as a will to power among ecclesiastics is soon aware that he has said the wrong thing. Yet how foolish it is to pretend that it is not there. For all churchmen by virtue of the very commission laid upon them to bring God to men are specially exposed to the temptation to give divine significance to what is only too human in their lives. The Catholic priest can turn cheap wine into the blood of Christ, the Protestant minister at the end of some vapid and ill-prepared discourse can say 'May the Lord add His blessing to the preaching of His word'. Are not all of us who are ordained to bring the Gospel of Christ to men not especially exposed to the temptation of saying however unconsciously 'Le bon Dieu, c'est moi' and of going on to canonise our thoughts, our prejudices and our actions, our neuroses and our imperialistic drives? The late H. R. Mackintosh used to warn his students, 'Always remember that those who dislike you may not dislike Christ'. More salutary advice could hardly be given to those about to be ordained. The temptation to imperialism is one of the professional hazards of the ordained. All the more reason for the Ecumenical Movement to say quite plainly what its watchword of the one church means. Does it mean, 'Let us all quit being ecclesiastical thugs' or 'Let us all grovel to the biggest ecclesiastical thug'?

On the claim to exclusiveness and why it finds a lodging with the Christian heart, something must be said also. There are those not unfriendly to Christianity who see in exclusiveness something inherent in Christianity, one side of that religion though undeniably the worse side. It was, I think, Simone Weil who said that the two words which kept her from being a Christian were *anathema sit*. And these words were spoken by St. Paul.

Karl Jaspers too is quite explicit in contending that a claim to exclusiveness is the seamy side of Christianity. Few philosophers can have spoken more highly of Christianity than Jaspers. He looks at Biblical religion, with its refusal to find anything common or unclean and its demand for truth in the inward parts, even as in the book of Job, at the cost of a satisfactory apologetic. And he finds in it one main source of modern science. Again, Jaspers looks at Europe where alone the insights of what he calls the Axial Era have developed into the scientific-technological era. Those who wish to play a part in science or technology must go to a university in Europe or to one founded by Europeans or by those educated by Europeans. And Jaspers finds the key to much of the greatness of Europe in Christianity. For the polarities (the metaphor is that of the positive and negative poles of an electric charge) which characterise Europe, such fruitful polarities as those between Church and State, between Christianity and Humanism, between Latin and Germanic nations, find their pattern in the equally fruitful polarities of Christianity. For behind the obvious polarity of Catholic and Protestant lie the polarities of the Bible itself, the polarity between the religion of the prophet and the religion of the priest, that between the Gospel of the Synoptics and the Gospel of John, that between the Epistles of Paul and the Epistle of James. Further Christianity, though in this its practice has lagged behind its precept, is the religion of love. That being so, it has enjoined on those who incline towards one pole the duty of seeking to understand those who incline towards the other, an exercise of love which has resulted in the enrichment of both parties.

So much for the credit side of Christianity. Its debit side Jaspers finds in exclusiveness. Of this Jaspers has several things to say. The first is that what I believe absolutely, that of what I may say as Luther said: 'Here I stand, I can do no other thing,' does not admit of universal proof[1]. And that holds too of its expression in word, dogma, cult and rite. Next this exclusiveness has in practice meant putting a halo round the will to power, cruelty and the desire to destroy. Thirdly, this exclusiveness seems peculiar to the Biblical religions, including Islam. They alone seem to have gone in for religious wars, an Inquisition and the maxim, 'compel them to come in'. Jaspers does not think one can stand neutral to exclusiveness, for one cannot tolerate intolerance, a maxim only too unhappily demonstrated by the way in which the Nazi party was allowed to rise to power in the Weimar Republic. But in the last resort Jaspers does not consider that Christianity with its fruitful polarities and its demand for love, can in its essence be exclusive.

This sympathetic assessment of Christianity by one of the leading philosophers of this century cannot but make the reflective Christian think more about exclusiveness. Is it inherent in Christianity or is it incompatible with its real nature? It is easy to see the argument for the first of these alternatives. By proclaiming Jesus Christ as unique, is the Christian not committed to exclusiveness? This may seem true as long as we stick to the concepts of uniqueness and exclusiveness. But the matter looks different when we pass from concepts to facts. If, that is, we consider first the Cross of Christ as a unique revelation of forgiving, suffering, love and then go on to consider the horrors of the Inquisition or, for that matter, of the Protestant battle cry: 'Christ Jesus and no quarter,' it is hard to resist the conclusion that we have passed from one thing to another quite different. The transition, to be blunt, is from the divine not just to the human but to the damnable.

We have, indeed, to face the question put by Jaspers, whether a claim to exclusiveness is not really incompatible with love and therefore with Christianity. After all the real point of belonging

1. In another very striking passage Jaspers contrasts Galileo and Bruno both of whom fell foul of the inquisition. Galileo recanted and was spared, Bruno refused to recant and was executed. Which did right? Jaspers' answer is 'Both'. For the truth for which Galileo stood was a scientific truth which can be proved and therefore need not be witnesses, and the truth for which Bruno stood was a religious truth which cannot be proved and therefore can only be witnessed to.

to an exclusive club, regiment, society or church, is that it enables you to look down on other people. This is incompatible with loving them, and when Jesus found any of His disciples taking up an exclusive attitude to their brethren, He promptly told them off. It is a negative and not very laudable attitude towards one's fellow men and naturally those who take it up do not admit that this is what they are doing when they lay claim to exclusiveness. But they blame others for doing the same thing. Thus Englishmen who practise financial segregation in their schools are quite ready to blame Southern Americans for practising racial segregation in theirs.

It is mercifully true that apart perhaps from Spain, civilised countries to-day would not tolerate the worst forms of ecclesiastical exclusiveness rightly condemned by Jaspers. If the Aufklärung and laicism have played their part in bringing about this happier state of secularism, then Christians ought to be grateful to them. A certain amount of contemporary claim to exclusiveness seems to be not so much harmful as just distinctly odd, a curious psychological condition so violent as to preclude even the use of certain names. Two instances of this may be given. In his recent contribution to ecumenicity, *The Loss of Unity*, [1]. Mr. Hoffman Nickerson has a chapter on Calvin. In the course of this he refers to Calvin, eleven times, not by his name but as 'The Devil-Worshipper'. On the jacket of his book we are told that Mr. Nickerson, an Anglo-Catholic who once advised Lord Halifax in his unity conversations with Cardinal Mercier, is an American historian of some note. I am not uncritical of Calvin either as a theologian or a man and indeed can no more accept his doctrine of double predestination than Professor Barth can. Even so I cannot understand why anyone trained as a historian should be unable to do this long deceased Frenchman the common courtesy of referring to him by his name instead of by a term of abuse. Obviously it must mean a lot to Mr. Nickerson to have a low opinion of Calvin.

So in *The British Churches Today*, [2]. a book by no means unfriendly to ecumenicity, Mr. Kenneth Slack mentions the

1. Sidgwick & Jackson, 1961.
2. S.C.M. 1961.

unwillingness of Anglo-Catholic journals to refer to the Church of Scotland by that name. One can only point out that the English Parliament recognised it by that title before it recognised a Mr. Washington as President of the United States. To be consistent the journals of which Mr. Slack speaks should refer to Mr. Lyndon Johnson as the leader of the rebellious American colonists.

With all this we have entered into the field of pleasant nuttiness. It is indeed one of the faults of the Ecumenical Movement that it urges churches which have largely shed their nuttiness to take seriously the nuttiness of those which have not. It is particularly alarming when one hears Ecumenicals stressing that laymen must be educated. It never occurs to them that laymen may have a healthier attitude to nuttiness than they have.

If we may venture a sentence which will provide Ecumenicals with a suitable place to write a violent comment in the margin of this book, for the moment we have come far enough. We have seen some of the harm done by the failure to analyse the term 'oneness' and in particular the failure to recognise that the will to power and the claim to exclusiveness are now and have always been factors in the ecclesiastical situation. So far we have spoken in general terms. It now remains to speak in more specific ones and to show how the factors to which we have drawn attention have actually operated in the relation between two churches both in the past and the present. The relation with which I am going to deal is that between the Church of Scotland and the Church of England. The reasons for selecting this particular inter-church relation are first that it is the one I am most competent to write about, and second that one thesis of this book is that what passes itself off as ecumenicity in English speaking countries is very largely Anglican imperialism, a phenomenon not unconnected with English nationalism.

What I propose to do is to talk about Anglo-Scottish ecclesiastical relations at four key periods, the first of which is the Reformation and the last of which is the present day. It is impossible to do this without bringing in the part played by the power factor. Thus the Scottish Reformation was an English strategic necessity, a point perhaps not markedly emphasised either by the Scottish church leaders or by the Archbishop of Canterbury in their speeches on the fourth anniversary of that event. But I shall try not to overemphasise the power factor and to show how it connects with other factors.

It is clearly impossible to write about Anglo-Scottish church relations without writing about England and Scotland. For one thing the Church of England is one of the great indigenous churches of Christendom, for another, one has to raise the question whether certain pathological features of English and Scottish life are connected with ecclesiastical developments. I shall try and write about England and Scotland impartially. One can only do this, however, by applying the same standards to Englishmen and to Scotsmen alike. If loyalty to his country's institutions is a good thing in an Englishman, then it is a good thing in a Scotsman. If treason, committed for money, is a bad thing in an Englishman, then it is a bad thing in a Scotsman.

Now this attempt at impartiality, while it might commend itself to such great Englishmen as Edmund Burke and, in our own day, Sir Arthur Bryant,[1] will not commend itself to those Englishmen who cannot really envisage that there are other countries which have other institutions and traditions than theirs—the kind of Englishman, for instance, whom one still hears saying that America has no history. Nor will it commend itself to the vast bulk of upper middle class Scotsmen who have reached the curious synthetic judgment that English institutions are U, Scottish institutions are non-U.

The kind of thinking to which these two groups are committed excludes any impartial comparison between Englishmen and Scotsmen. It is best illustrated by the thinking of a Nazi in a conversation which Mr. Shirer records in his *Berlin Diary*. The conversation took place during the First Finnish War. 'A German friend said (to an American), "Isn't it terrible what the Finns are doing, taking on Russia? It's utterly wrong". When the American remonstrated, that after all, the Finns were only doing what you would expect all decent Germans to do if they

---

1. See his article on the General Assembly of the Church of Scotland in the *Sunday Times*

got into the same fix—namely defending their liberty and independence—the Nazi retorted, "But Russia is Germany's friend." '

Mr. Shirer comments 'in other words for a German to defend his country's life and independence is right. For a Finn to do the same thing is wrong, because it disturbs Germany's relations with Russia.' This is exactly the same as the view that it is all wrong for an Englishman to despise the institutions of his country, but it is all right for a Scotsman to despise those of his. The virtues of the Herrenvoek are not those of the Minderrassiges Volk. This is pure racialism.

Any attempt to give an impartial account of Anglo-Scottish relations involves a rejection of this essentially Nazi point of view. One can reject this view point and yet recognise that it plays a large part on both sides of the Border and indeed that it is an influential factor in the thinking of the Ecumenical Movement in the English speaking world.

But before we deal with England and Scotland, we must first write of a greater than either or both, Europe. Only in the light of Europe can the phenomenon of English nationalism be understood.

7

Europe

IN his review in the *Listener* of the first number of the periodical, *Encounter*, A. J. P. Taylor, the Oxford historian, wrote about the five philosophers whose names appeared on the cover in the following words. 'All five are . . . . . . philosophers in a now outmoded sense. That is, they all pontificate about man's duty and his place in society. One of them is also a brilliant writer, but this is an accident. His name is Bertrand Russell. The unreadable four it is unnecessary to name.'[1] In a letter to the editor of the same journal, Stephen Spender remarked: 'It is to the interest of Mr. Taylor's reputation as a university teacher and universal broadcaster of his views to name the unnameable ones. They are: Karl Jaspers, Salvador de Madariága, Jacques Maritain and Reinhold Niebuhr.'[2]

In the last chapter we connected reluctance to mention a name with a degree of strong feeling. And no doubt this distinguished English historian in refusing to name these four un-English writers was expressing not only his own passionate conviction but that of English philosophers of the period. Yet perhaps it was a pity that such a view should be held so strongly in 1953 by so many influential Englishmen. Reinhold Niebuhr's insights on power we have already availed ourselves of. And Jaspers, the philosopher of Europe, could perhaps have taught Englishmen that there are other aspects of Europe than the economic expediencies or inexperiences of a Common Market.

Some of these aspects are very simple. Geographically Europe

1. *Listener*. 8.10.53.
2. *Listener*. 15.10.53.

is a peninsula with an island attached. Only the fact that we hang our maps with the north at the top keeps us from seeing its similarity to Greece and Italy, or for that matter to the Malay peninsula with the island of Singapore. Behind Europe, as behind these other peninsulas lies a Heartland inaccessible to sea power.

The hazards of a peninsula are clear to see. After the Greek city states had indulged in their final and bloody luxury of the Peloponnesian War, Philip of Macedon came down their peninsula and took them all, Athens, Sparta, the lot. Hannibal countered the fact that sea power was against him by crossing first the narrow straits of Gibraltar and then the Alps, in order to carry out the same manoeuvre against the Romans. He nearly overran the Italian peninsula. Against a similar Japanese move down the Malay peninsula in 1942 the great sea fortress of Singapore was helpless.

Historically the peninsula of Europe has not been spared a like predicament. All through the Middle Ages, Europe was besieged. The besiegers got as far as Vienna; more than that, by moving along the North African coast and then crossing into Spain, they took the garrison in the rear. The Crusades were unsuccessful attempts to raise the siege. Then in 1497 the siege was raised when Vasco da Gama sailed round Africa into the Indian Ocean and took the besiegers in the rear. From then on the Europeans never looked back. Here is how the Cambridge Modern History (Vol. 1, p.26) describes the sequel, 'Ever since da Gama's great voyage Southern and Eastern Asia, comprising then as now the most populous nations on the globe, have been gradually falling under the sway of the European powers, who have first appropriated their foreign trade, making permanent settlements on their coasts in order to secure it, thence advancing to controlling their administration and usurping their government, and in some varying degree have succeeded in the more difficult task of gradually changing their habits of life and thought'. If anything the passage is an understatement for in addition to their exploits in Southern and Eastern Asia, the Europeans have colonised the Americas, have developed art, science, music, philosophy to an amazing extent and have in addition still retained enough energy to fight wars with one another. The enormous burst of European vitality is something quite incredible. Equally amazing is the fact that it has stopped dead, quite suddenly, in the lifetime of those still middle-aged. The words of the Cambridge Modern History, true when they were written in 1902 are completely out of date now. The European sortie is over now—it is in reverse. The British have left India, the Dutch have left Indonesia, the French have left Indo-China and Algeria. So much for the South and East Asia of which the Cambridge Modern History spoke. Elsewhere the change is as marked. At the end of the First World War, the Americans walked out of the Peace Conference and the show went on. The Russians weren't even asked. At the end of the Second World War there couldn't be a peace Conference because the Americans and the Russians didn't agree. We have here a truly momentous factor. For the first time for many hundreds of years the destinies of the inhabitants of Europe rest with men who live outside its bounds in Washington or Moscow.

This brilliant and sustained burst of European vitality so recently ended, sets us in a complex of problems, some of which it raises, others of which it helps to solve. Before going on to the problems, let us first notice how Jaspers defines more precisely the European achievement. We can do this by amplifying the account we gave of his views in the previous chapter. In his *Origin and Goal of History*, he makes it clear that for him the key point of history is the period from 800 to 200 B.C. which he calls the Axial Era. This is the age of Confucious, Lao-Tse, Buddha, Homer, Socrates, Plato and the Hebrew prophets. But it is not just an age singularly rich in great men. It is a period in which something happened to mankind. It is the period when man, for the first time, became aware of himself and of his limits. Radical questions were asked; religious, traditions and institutions, which previously had been simply accepted were now examined. For the first time man stood outside the life that he lived in religion and in society and criticised it. He found himself doing things in a certain way because tradition and custom had laid it down that they should be done in that way.

But he now asked himself if there weren't other possible ways in which he could do these things.

The Axial Era was therefore a period of criticism, of fluidity, and indeed of revolution. The kind of activity which went on in it is probably most familiar to us as it was exemplified in the work of the Sophists and Socrates and Plato as we see in their examination of the traditional Greek ideas of citizenship and conduct and in the reforming zeal with which Plato censors the immoral stories of the gods which have been handed down in Greek mythology from the days before the Axial Era. It is also familiar to us in the utterances of the Hebrew prophets when they criticise the religious cultus. When Isaiah handed on the command, 'Bring me no more vain oblations,' he was showing himself a revolutionary. In an earlier age men had brought oblations without considering whether they were vain or not. But if we are most familiar with the ferment of the Axial Era as it went on in Greece and Palestine, we must remember that the same sort of thing was going on quite independently in India and China.

It is true that the Axial Era is not the first of those epochs in which man seems, as it were, to make a new start. Jaspers singles out two such advances prior to it. The first is the Promethean Age, the period of the discovery of speech, of fire and of tools. The second is the period of what Jaspers calls the old high cultures, the civilisations of Egypt, Babylon and Assyria. Jaspers does not give any ultimate explanations how these civilisations began but he notes that they arose in great river valleys out of, or along with, the scope given for co-ordination of effort by the need to check the floods of the river and to use it for irrigation. They grew up with the discovery of writing, without which such large scale co-ordination of effort is, at anyrate, very difficult. But in these old high cultures there is something lacking which was to appear in the Axial Era. Traditions, customs, religions are not criticised, they are simply accepted. Man is content to fit himself into a pattern. He does not stand outside the pattern and ask whether it is the best pattern for him.

In examining the traditional pattern of life and asking whether

it was the best pattern for him, man was forced to examine himself and the problem he found to be a baffling one. Out of this
uncertainty about himself, this inward contradiction and
limitation, arose a new need for religion. But if the activity of
the Axial Era made man aware of his limitations, it also gave
him a new and intoxicating sense of his possibilities. For the
criticism of the traditional pattern of his life involved the
appreciation of alternative possible patterns and that wide
vista gave human life a breadth which it had not hitherto possessed. It is true that the Axial Era was not always ultimately
revolutionary. Sometimes it retained and venerated the myths
handed down to it and felt a loyalty to the institutions which it
had inherited. But even when, after examination, the institutions
and religions were retained, the very fact that they had been
examined had perhaps altered them subtly.

One curious feature of the Axial Era is that it occurred more
or less simultaneously and independently in three different
parts of the earth's surface, in the West, in India and in China.
Equally curious is the fact that in one of these areas and one
only, the West, the activity had taken place which has led to the
fourth new start of mankind, the scientific-technological era
in which we are living to-day. About this era, Jaspers has no
unduly high hopes. Inferior in depth to the Axial Era, it can
better be compared to the discovery of speech, forge and tools
which marks the Promethean Age. But it came to birth in
Europe and Europe alone.

We have dealt with Jaspers' views in some detail because they
help us to define more clearly the European achievement. In
achieving what he did European man incurred guilt. Some of
his more ignoble activities, like the slave trade, are quite re-
voltingly horrible. Taken together they can be summed up as
what is now called colonisation, the unjustifiable claim to
enjoy a higher standard of living than other races. But there is
more to being a European than just having a guilt complex. It
is because they have an appreciation of the positive side of the
European four hundred sortie that not a few Frenchmen, Germans and Italians tend to think of themselves primarily as
Europeans. Why they should do this at a time when the English

Press was still tending to reserve the term for the more unpleasant white settlers in Kenya is a natural question. The
answer is perhaps that the mainland countries had all known
occupation. They did not end the 1939–45 war with a nominal
victory, the pretence of equality with the U.S. and Russia,
intact institutions and the consequent comforting illusion that
the 19th century was still on. They knew that Europe had been
destroyed. The cause of the destruction was fairly obvious.
Europe to its credit had refused to lie down under the union imposed on it by Hitler whose doctrines of racialism ran counter
to that synthesis of Christianity and Stoic Natural Law which
has formed the spiritual backbone of Europe. But to over-
throw Hitler was impossible without massive Russian and
American help. The war ended in 1945 with the occupation by
these two countries of a Europe which no longer contained within itself a great power. Europe had had its Peloponnesian War.

But with a sense of the catastrophe went a sense of what the
European achievement had been and a will to rebuild Europe
on a less fratricidal basis. It is that will with its blend of idealism
and realism that is basic in the European scene to-day.

If we turn now to the relations between the peninsula of
Europe and the adjacent island, we find an interesting anomaly.
One basic principle of Geopolitics laid down by Mackinder is
that sea power tends to pass from an island to a peninsular
power. The reason for this is that the peninsular power, unlike the island power, can take in more land. This provides it
with more timber to build more ships and more manpower to
form crews for them. In the end the expandable peninsula will
build up a fleet sufficient to overcome that of the more restricted
island base. Thus the island power of Crete wanes. The Greek
peninsular states wax.

To this maxim of Geopolitics there is one notable exception,
as Mackinder notes. It is that of England and Europe. For many
hundred years England held sea power and defied any power
based on the European peninsula to wrest it from her. Two
things, according to Mackinder, have enabled England to do
this. The first is the extraordinary agricultural and industrial
wealth of England and the fact that the Industrial revolution

got under way quicker there than elsewhere. A much richer island can still manage to out-build, out-man and out-gun the fleet of a peninsula. That this is part of the secret of England's long retention of power one can hardly doubt. As Mackinder truly says the flag of the Royal Navy is rightly the St. George's Cross. Had England been a mountainous country like that of the Highlands of Scotland the history of the Royal Navy and the history of Europe would have been very different.

The other factor to which Mackinder ascribes England's retention of sea power is even more interesting. It is that the policy of the London Government has always been to secure the balance of power in Europe, i.e. to keep the peninsula divided. The Europeans are thus weakened and so rendered incapable of wresting sea power from the island. That Mackinder was right in finding the balance of power a keystone of island policy is shown by the fact that whenever that policy has broken down the London Government has always been in a critical situation. Sometimes the crisis is brought about by Europe being united by force, as by Napoleon and by Hitler. But sometimes it is brought about when the peninsular powers come together by treaty, as was the case in 1558 and 1960. In the first of these crises the English Government called the Church of Scotland into being, in the second E.F.T.A. Unlike as these two institutions appear to be, they resemble one another in being meant as a defence of English interests against those of the leading continental powers. But the second crisis is not yet resolved and it is doubtful if the English nationalism of the New Elizabethan Age will be as successful as that of the Old Elizabethan Age.

Before we raise moral issues, it is as well to state the relation between England and the peninsula of Europe quite boldly in terms of the power equations of a Realpolitik. England has maintained its power by doing its best to keep the peninsula of Europe divided. The peninsula of Europe is now consciously seeking to restore its power by uniting permanently both economically and politically. This is the current and very acute crisis for English nationalism.

When we try dispassionately to introduce morality into the

Realpolitik, it is not altogether easy to see which side it supports. On the one hand, the English policy has been admirably suited to enable Englishmen to believe, and, sometimes, as in 1939, to believe correctly in the rightness of their cause. If you help the little 'un to fight against the big 'un, you inevitably appear in a good light, and rightly so, unless perhaps the big 'un and the little 'un would have been living at peace with one another, if it hadn't been for you. Certainly the English attitude to European unity is reflected less in the words of Mr. Churchill's Zürich speech (made when he was in opposition) advocating Franco-German rapprochement than in such actions as the inadequate offer of one and a half divisions which prevented the European army from coming into being, and the refusal to join in the negotiations which led to the Treaty of Rome.

On the other, the European side, Frenchmen and Germans who think that reconciliation between their two countries is a good thing which ought to have come a lot earlier, are bound to have a critical view of the English doctrine of the balance of power. Further, it may well be urged that Europe stands for something, that it is more important than any single nation and that it must be allowed to find the unity on which its future depends. Hence with the successful formation of the Common Market and the subsequent desire of the British Government to join it, the Europeans were faced with a much deeper question than the many very difficult technical economic questions which also arose. Were the English really in sympathy with the European spirit? Or were they seeking to join the community perhaps not to break it up but to keep it at the economic stage and prevent it achieving the fullness of political unity that its most dedicated sponsors envisaged for it? The fact that the verdict that the English were not sufficiently European was rather ironically given by the not unnationalistic General de Gaulle should not blind us to the difficulty of the European dilemma. In the light of English nationalism and the history of English attitudes to European unity, is it wise to take the island into membership of the community?

In the last resort the criterion of nationality is existential. A man is what he conceives himself to be. At the beginning of the

Civil War, General Robert E. Lee refused the command of the United States Army because he felt himself to be a Virginian rather than an American, whereas Federal generals, some of them actually from the South, felt themselves to be Americans rather than Vermonters. Do the English think of themselves as Europeans rather than as English? Future events will provide the answer to that question. But from the standpoint of the present, three factors seem to point against the English being good members of a European union. First the equanimity with which they have parted with the British Empire seems to suggest that all they really cared for was England and not the great land mass painted red on turn-of-the-century maps. Secondly, it is very doubtful if their union with Scotland in 1707 has ever meant anything to them. Scotsmen who become enraged by English usage (particularly in moments of emotional exaltation) of 'England' and 'the Queen of England' for their country and their monarch would be better employed in drawing the implications of this usage. One of these is that Englishmen do not think of themselves as British in any sense other than as English. Finally, and this is one of the themes of this book, the idea of a union as conceived in recent years by that indigenous English institution, the Anglican church, is not a little reminiscent of the way in which the spider unites with the fly.

PART THREE

Anglo-Scottish Ecclesiastical Relations

The Past

8

Reformation and Realpolitik

We saw in the last chapter that if the leading continental powers come together, an extremely awkward situation arises for the London Government. Such a situation occurred in the year 1558. In that year Valois France and Hapsburg Spain signed the treaty of Cateau-Cambresis. Both these were Catholic powers, whereas England had for some years shaken off the allegiance of the Pope. The situation, already dangerous, by reason of continental unification, was rendered the more menacing by the fact that England had a Catholic Scotland on her northern frontier. In the circumstances it is not surprising that the English Secretary Cecil should resolve to help the Scots Reformers 'first with money, then with arms, then with men.' It is not surprising indeed that the Scottish Reformation followed in 1560. From the standpoint of Realpolitik, the Scottish Reformation was the English strategic reaction to a very tricky situation indeed.

The trouble about the Scottish Reformation from the historical viewpoint of the ordinary man is that it lends itself too easily to melodrama. The slaying of Cardinal Beaton, the interviews between Knox and Mary, Queen of Scots, the murders of the latter's secretary and husband and her own death at the hands of the English headsman all tend to draw the spotlight on themselves and away from less obvious and less emotionally coloured factors. Actually so much takes place in accordance with the power equations of a *Realpolitik* that it is as well to begin by noting some of the moral and spiritual factors involved.

The Reformation in Scotland was part of a wider movement initiated when Luther nailed his theses to the church door at Wittenberg. To those who accepted them, his stand must have seemed a moral protest against an institution which appeared to do rather well out of the common sorrows of man, the fears that beset him in the fact of the unknown and the love that he has for those dear to him. His teaching was brought from Germany to Scotland by Patrick Hamilton in 1527. Too early and too weak a Reformer to be a successful one, Hamilton was spared the compromises with. power which are the price of success. His death by burning at St. Andrews in 1528 made him the first of those who in Scotland were to be victims of the idea of the One Church and of the inability of Christians to recognise in love the otherness of other Christians. Their number of either side is mercifully small. In spite of, or because of, its crudity and lawlessness there is in Scotland nothing comparable to the cold-blooded horrors of Torquemeda's Inquisition or even on the Protestant side, to Calvin's execution of Servetus.

Hamilton's death at the hand of the ruling church must inevitably have led men to question the moral structure of that institution. The answers can hardly have been satisfactory. The bishoprics held *in commendam* for the relatives of the king, legitimate or otherwise, or else in the hands of the great feudal families; the exactions of the church felt—if we are to believe the *Satire of the Three Estaits*—to be a grievous burden by the common man; the cardinal with his flock of bastard children are factors which explain a good deal. The reactions of quiet thinking men who care somewhat about morals—and among such we may without undue charity reckon at least some of the simple country gentlemen and burgh merchants who supported the Reformation—can at times of crisis be quite a factor. This happened at least twice with unfavourable results for the unfortunate Queen, once after her marriage with Bothwell and again after the massacre of St. Bartholomew. To note that is not necessarily to justify it, for moralistic reactions can be both short-sighted and vindictive. But the fact remains that nobody who had grown up in Scotland put up much of a fight for the old church and Protestants found it easy to have the sometimes questionable impression that theirs was the cause of right.

Revolutions, however, are in the main not brought about by quiet men who care about morals but by those who have power or know how to seize it. In Scotland, a feudal outcrop in a Renaissance world, power lay predominantly in the hands of the nobles. Unlike England, the country had not experienced Wars of the Roses where rival notabilities had obligingly laid each other low for the crown to emerge in the end as *tertium gaudens*. If the Reformation was to succeed, the nobles, or a majority of them had to be won for the Protestant faith.

In the circumstances it is natural to argue that the nobles were won over to the Reformation by the prospect of acquiring the church lands. As the latter were extensive, the bait was a considerable one and there is no doubt that it was what attracted a man like the Earl of Morton. On the other hand, Professor Lee of Princeton, in his admirable biography of the Earl of Moray, has argued that the latter was won by the teaching of Knox to a genuine acceptance of Protestantism. This impression is confirmed by one's suspicion that Moray was so competent an operator in the field of real estate that he was quite capable of getting enough land for himself anyway. And in this connection it must be remembered that even before the Reformation the nobles had their own ways of tapping the revenues of the church lands.

There was, however, another financial inducement which could lead the nobles to adopt the Protestant cause and with that come to the second and greater power factor in the Scottish Reformation, the English Government. If the nobles could establish or ruin the Reformed church, the English Government could buy the nobles. For the English the time was indeed opportune. After the two military disasters of Flodden and Solway Moss, some of the Scottish nobles began to doubt the wisdom of the traditional policy of friendship with France and enmity with England. The seeds of doubt thus sown were judiciously nourished by bribes from the English Government which had now broken with Rome. The prisoners-of-war from the battle of the Solway returned to Scotland with English pensions in their pockets. For them, at anyrate, the reappraisal of foreign policy was not to be too agonising. And a like douceur was to come the way of other Scotsmen of influence who subsequently showed themselves willing to adapt their international and religious thinking to the needs of England's strategy. For the English statesmen there can be little criticism. Compared with the fire-eating Plantagenet, Edward I, they showed themselves at once moderate and astute. So many centuries had been wasted in battling with the Scots, was it not more efficacious to buy them instead? It certainly was. The one relapse into sabre-rattling by Henry VIII and Somerset had the (for the English) quite disastrous effect of driving the Scots to send their Queen to spend the formative years of her life at the French Court. Apart from that one setback English troops were to have the new experience of getting a welcome in Scotland when they were there strictly by invitation of groups of Protestant nobles. If the Scottish nobles were to find it easier to get English military aid than William the Silent did in a struggle of which the tolerant Protestantism of to-day can be prouder than of anything which happened in 16th century Scotland, perhaps the reason is just that the English Government was not foolish enough to embark on a Protestant jehad. But Scotland was different. Encirclement and a war on two fronts are possibilities that no sensible government wishes to become actual. From the English standpoint Scotland had to become Protestant.

Such was the comparatively simple framework of the Scottish Reformation struggle within which a number of characters played roles whose complexity can only be indicated in a sentence. There was Moray who gave a lifetime of statesman-like devotion to the Queen of a foreign country; Kirkcaldy of Grange who defended one castle against the French and their friends and another against the English and theirs; George Buchanan, whose philosophical vindication of the chronic anarchy of the nobles, the *De Jure Regni apud Scotos*, was to become one of the great textbooks of democracy; Maitland of Lethington, for whom union between England and Scotland meant so much that in the end he seemed to imagine that it could be forced on the English by French or Spanish intervention. Even Bothwell, casual in his sexual relationships—a matter in which he had an unfortunate example from his uncle, the Bishop of Moray—and involved in a murder which may have taken the unpleasant form of strangling a sick man, is by no means pure villain. Kirkcaldy, in a letter to an Englishman, wrote of the Queen's attitude to Bothwell in language which if sour, is not without colour. She would, wrote the Fife laird, 'go with him to the world's end in a white petticoat ere she leave him.' If so, the reason was perhaps that he was the only Scotsman of note who had given unswerving loyalty to her mother and herself. It must have been a relief to have someone about the place who was not in touch with the English ambassador.

Whether the Queen herself was tainted with treason so far as a sovereign can be is an arguable point. If before her first marriage she secretly signed away the liberties of Scotland to France much can be said in extenuation for a young girl living far from home in the most powerful court in Europe. But compassion for her fate can go with recognition that for her Scotland was not so much a cause as a means to an end, the end being the English crown. If Elizabeth gave the Englishmen a pride in being English, Mary did not give anything analogous to Scotsmen. And ultimately for lack of that in high places the country perished as a national state.

Of Knox many have written but perhaps none so well as his English biographer, Lord Eustace Percy. The key to much in him lies in his doctrine of the Lord's Supper and in his acceptance of Old Testament categories. If the former led him to believe that the Mass was idolatory the latter warned him that an idolatrous Queen brought divine retribution not just on herself but on the people over whom she ruled. A doctor would soon run out of politeness toward a typhoid carrier who refused his advice and Knox's interviews with the Queen and his references to her are marked as plain speaking which on occasion did rather more than verge on rudeness.

There have been other Christian divines—and not just in Knox's denomination—who may have rather enjoyed the exercise of power. Indeed the ecclesiastic may have his desire to get his way strengthened by a quite genuine conviction that what he is seeking is the will of God. What was distinctive about Knox was not that he was domineering and intolerant—there is little tolerance in the Old Testament—but that the power which he envisaged for himself and the other Scottish ministers was not so much sacerdotal or hierarchical as prophetic. To put the matter bluntly, they were to be able to tell off the monarch. True to his Old Testament outlook, Knox thought of himself as playing the role of Nathan to the sovereign's David. This was all right as long as the monarch was weak enough to have to accept the telling off and consequently Knox's Old Testament standpoint fitted very well with the pressures which the nobles and the English Government were able to put on the Scottish crown. But the harmony between the Knoxian theology and the political realities was not to last very long. The role of a David or a Hezekiah did not commend itself to the new King, James VI, who much preferred the less democratic New Testament teaching of Romans 13. During his Edinburgh period James succeeded in getting the English Government to transfer its support from the nobles to himself. How much this new arrangement meant to him is shown by the fact that he acquiesced when shortly afterwards his allies proceeded to execute his mother. When in 1603, James finally achieved his end and moved to London as King of England, he was able to deal drastically with the Kirk. Thus in 1606 he was able to summon to London, Andrew Melville, on whom the mantle of Knox had fallen, and other troublesome ministers. Once there they were subjected to an intensive course of Anglican sermons. Almost inevitably Romans 13 came up for exposition and it is reported that the Bishop of Chichester proved from some silver trumpets in the Book of Numbers that the right of convening and discharging ecclesiastical assemblies lay with the King, which was a very nasty blow at the powers of the Scots General Assembly. Melville remained unconvinced by all this and shortly afterwards treated the Archbishop of Canterbury to one of those displays of plain speaking with which he had been accustomed to regale the King of Scotland. But now he had the King of England to deal with and James had him sent to the Tower for three years after which he was allowed to end his days as an exile in Sudan. With the fall of Melville the Knoxian synthesis of theology and political realities finally fell apart. It had carried the seeds of disintegration within herself. For Knox's Old Testament conception of the role of the church was incompatible with the union with England just as his far reaching schemes of education were incompatible with the rapacity of the nobles.

The struggle thus fought out has had its repercussions in our own day. When in 1937, during the German church struggle, Karl Barth came to give the Gifford Lectures at Aberdeen, he was to welcome the fact that the Scots Confession of 1560 took the commandment 'thou shalt not kill' to imply the repression of tyranny. And when in 1951 the issue of the treason or otherwise of the 20th July conspirators against Hitler came before the German Courts in the Remer trial, the Scots Confession was cited in their support. To those who prefer Bonhoeffer to Knox and Beck and Stauffenberg (the latter a Catholic) to Moray and Morton, such citation might seem to be the justification of good men by the apologia of those less worthy. After all, is it not absurd to class Mary, Queen of Scots and her mother, Mary of Guise with Hitler? In actual fact neither of these women came near to being a tyrant. If they had the inclination to be one, they did not have the power. At times one feels that those who resisted them assumed rather gratuitously that they had the inclination. It may be, however, that the fate of Hus did not dispose Protestant subjects unduly to trust a Catholic sovereign. And as the years went by both women were seen not in themselves but as the weak bridgeheads of a tyranny that was to manifest itself in the atrocities of Alva's army and the massacre of St. Bartholomew. Fear may sometimes have led the Scottish Protestants to say and do things that were misguided and even cruel. But the fear was not altogether groundless.

9

Aftermath of a Reformation

We have traced the genesis of the Scottish Reformation back to what for the English Government was the threatening power situation of 1558. Similar power factors determined the different course taken by the Reformation in the two countries. The reason why the Church of England became episcopalian and the Church of Scotland presbyterian is not that sound theological thinking was carried on in the one country and unsound in the other. Theological thinking has very little to do with the case (except to find spurious justifications for the winning side). The real factor is to be found in the difference of the power structures of the two countries during the sixteenth century. This can be seen as soon as we recollect that because of their insistence on the idea of the One Church, the Roman ecclesiastical authorities considered it right to liquidate anyone who seemed to them to be starting a second one. For those who broke with Rome in the sixteenth century to remain alive was therefore a top priority. Survival was achieved by getting on good terms with those who had power and who were willing to afford protection—at a price. In England, a highly developed Renaissance state, power lay in the hands of the crown. The Monarch was willing to protect the new church at a price. His price was that his views were to be what went in the new church and that they were to be enforced by his own nominees in key positions. The two Anglican positions of the Sovereign as head of the church and an episcopate thus follow inevitably from the logic of the situation. It is no doubt more respectable if they can be bolstered up by what still to-day sometimes passes for theology. But they would have been there anyway. The Tudors just like Hitler during the German Church Struggle were bound to favour Bishops rather than General Assemblies.

Sixteenth century Scotland, on the other hand, was a feudal anachronism in a Renaissance world. Power lay in the hands not of the Crown but of the nobles, Argyll, Glencairn and the rest. To them converts to the new faith naturally turned in an understandable desire to remain alive. Here again protection was given and given at a price. The price was a say in the government of the Reformed church. When the first General Assembly met the feudal magnates quietly drew in their chairs and joined in. Again their presence could be left to be justified by the strained laws of exegesis. Its real justification lay in the more basic law that if you rely on someone to shoot you out of a situation he will expect to have some say in determining the kind of situation you are going to get yourself into. If the proto-types of English bishops are government stooges, the prototypes of Scots elders are guys with guns.

It is hardly necessary to add that this description fits neither bishops nor elders today. The fact is that both the Church of England and the Church of Scotland have developed as organic institutions to meet the needs of the changing centuries. It would be a pity if they were not allowed to continue their de-velopment, each in its own way. Not that there is much danger of Englishmen allowing outsiders to interfere with one of their institutions.

The general pattern before us is thus one of ecclesiastical actions brought about by the reality of power structures. Those who held the power could in the nature of the case prevail upon divines to provide exegetical and theological justification for what they did. Indeed, sometimes, as in the case of James VI, they provided the theological justification themselves. This was all very good policy. For obviously if you want your own will to prevail quite the best thing to do is to try to persuade other people that it is in fact God's will. This is a technique still employed in ecclesiastical politics.

Nonetheless, if we are wise, we will not confuse the causes of ecclesiastical actions with what purport to be their theological and exegetical justifications. And it might be well if the latter were treated with a little more healthy disrespect in present-day ecumenical discussions. F. W. Maitland in treating of the habits of sixteenth century Scottish nobles remarked very fairly that 'The "bond" is no less a "bond" because it is styled a "covenant" and makes free with holy names.' And on the other hand the Divine Right of Kings remains an excellent device for enabling Charles I to get out of any obligations to anybody even if it also purports to be an exegesis of Romans 13. And if nobles and Kings can confuse the justification of their own power claims with pure theology, the same may be true of ecclesiastics. To become ordained is not necessarily to escape from one's desire for power. It may only serve to canonize it.

To point to the part played by power structures in bringing about ecclesiastical actions is not to deny that played by decision. We have to decide within the limits imposed by the power structures which dominate our environment but we can none-theless decide. We can decide how far we are to co-operate with the power structure, we can even decide to revolt against it though we will not do so successfully unless we ally ourselves with a stronger one. Some people indeed are able to choose what kind of power they will exercise. This kind of decision was made by Knox and it was a very fateful one for Anglo-Scottish rela-tions. Knox wanted power. In this he was like all ecclesiastics (for, after all, nobody compels them to be ecclesiastics.) What distinguishes him from the others is that, as we have seen, he preferred prophetic to hierarchical or sacerdotal power. That is to say, he sought power over the crown or executive rather than over the clergy or the laity. The power to which Knox aspired was more akin to that which the prophet Nathan exercised at the court of King David than to that which a Church of England bishop wields in his diocese or an Irish priest in his parish. This was indeed a fateful decision, for Kings while having no objection to divines bossing curates or ordinary citizens do not take kindly to being bossed themselves. Behind Knox's choice lay the insight that power was the thing which had to be controlled. Its demerit lay in his failure to see that the power to rebuke power, itself involved the temptations of power.

To these temptations Knox and his successors in the Scottish Church sometimes succumbed. In their public and private lecturing of the monarch they could be rude, tactless and diplomatically inept. They could also sometimes be right and they could always act as a brake on royal megalomania.

Such a cold blooded assessment of the power he sought for himself and the church would have been foreign to Knox. From him the whole thing followed from the Old Testament which he accepted as a blueprint for Scotland. As he remarked in a classic phrase 'Ahab was ane King and Jezebel was ane Queen'. The prophets had not been inhibited in handing out unpleasant statements to these monarchs and Knox would not accept the Secretary of State's view that these were singular motions of the Spirit of God which pertain nothing to this our present age.

On this central issue of the prophetic conception of power the early Scottish Reformed church stands or falls. To most of the other charges popularly made against it, it can supply a reasonably good defence. It contained within its ranks men like Buchanan and Melville whose international reputation for learning can hardly be equalled by many Scotsmen today. Its theology was not unduly repressive. Knox had, it is true, written a long and wearisome treatise on predestination. But predestination in the sixteenth century was simply the transposition into a theological key of the existential decision to shake off the power of the mediaeval church. Predestination asserted that the ultimate destiny of the believer lay in the hand of God alone. But the sting of the doctrine lay in what it denied. In the sixteenth century context the point of that statement lay in the fact that it declared redundant the church's pre-Reformation expensive mechanism for providing a better fate for the loved one after death.

In the field of conduct too the early Reformed Church of Scotland was within its limits refreshingly liberal. Augustine remained an authority for it and so it was unable to escape completely from his warped views on sex which are the common misfortune of all western churches. But Calvin had at least rejected Augustine's dreadful doctrine of the exclusion from heaven of unbaptised children and in this the Church of Scotland followed him. Further one consequence of the Reformation in Scotland was that from 1560 on and thus some three hundred years earlier than in England, the Scottish Law Courts granted decrees of divorce. If the Church of Scotland to-day has a less puritanical attitude on sex than the Church of England or the Roman Catholic Church the credit in large measure is due to the Reformers.

So much can be said in vindication of the Church of Scotland's standpoints. But we are still left with the question of Knox and Melville's prophetic conception of power. Was it a salutary check on absolutist power in church and state? Or did it render effective executive government impossible? How far is it responsible for the curious disloyalty syndrome which forms a feature of Scottish history up to and including the present, and makes it so different from that of England?

To these questions it is impossible to give 'yes' or 'no' answers. The justifications of the Church of Scotland's claim to prophetic power have been of considerable service to those fighting absolutism. We have seen how the Scots Confession of 1560 gave help to Barth seeking to arouse Christian opposition to Hitler in 1937 and to those who sought to clear the name of the 20th July conspirators at the Remer trial of 1951. The *De Jure Regni apud Scotos* of George Buchanan was in a sense written to justify the chronic and archaic anarchy of the Scottish nobles. But it was written by an extremely able man and it has become one of the great text books of democracy, all the more so because Buchanan's vindication of the acts of the Reformers and their party rests not so much on an arbitrary interpretation of scripture as on classical antiquity and what he considers to be the plain facts of human nature. For Buchanan the view of a collection of mediocrities is better than that of one semi-superman. And that, after all, is perhaps the best and most sober argument for parliamentary government or presbyterianism.

But this is to justify not so much the actions of the Kirk as the apologia for its actions. We can be impressed by the writings of those we would not have cared to live with. Certainly James VI found the Kirk hard to live with. As Mr. Willson has said he regarded 'The Scottish Reformation as an anti-monarchical revolt against constituted authority'. As Professor Lee points out James VI's own view was 'that a Christian King should be the Chief Governor of the Kirk . . . . . . have bishops under him, to hold all in order'. This is Anglicanism and in 1603 James took the logical step and went to London to be King there. From his point of view the move was a good one. 'Here I sit' wrote James in London in 1607 'and govern Scotland by my pen. I write and it is done, and by a clerk of the council I govern Scotland now, which other could not do by the sword.'

There is therefore a prima facie case against the Church of Scotland that it made executive government within Scotland impossible and thus made the country a province administered from London. This is a very serious charge, for what Englishman would care to have his country administered from Brussels, or worse still, from Bonn? It is reinforced by the fact that when during the Civil War the Church of Scotland played a leading part in determining the country's policy, its efforts ended in the ultimate debacle of enemy occupation.

If for the moment we leave the seventeenth century we can acquit the Church of Scotland of any undue share in the destruction of Scotland as a nation. It was not the Church of Scotland which drove James VI to London. The crown of England, that rich and highly developed Renaissance state, drew him like a magnet, quite apart from the troublesome nature of the Kirk. After all, it had drawn his mother before him. With both of them nationalism came a very poor second to dynastic ambition.

Again, the very fact that history does not yield the result that the power equations suggest, shows that Reformed Scotland was viable as a national state. One would expect the sixteenth century Church of Scotland to be Presbyterian or Episcopalian according as to whether the English pay cheque was made out to the nobles or to the crown. But in point of fact even after James VI got the English subsidy transferred to him there was a period when the Church of Scotland remained Presbyterian. Professor Maurice Lee has shown that this was due to James's chancellor, John Maitland. Maitland believed and was able to demonstrate that a modern executive could co-operate with a moderate Kirk. On Maitland's death, however, James who wanted from the church not so much co-operation as submission took over full control of policy and episcopacy followed.

10

Civil War and Scottish Imperialism

In the hundred and four years between 1603 and 1707 the names in Scottish Church history change but the real causal factors remain the same. On the one hand there is the King, secure and strong in his English base. For forty years the beggary of the Kirk's policy of union with England became more and more manifest. The black queen had become the white queen. A monarch who lived in London was not a monarch whom the Church of Scotland could tell off. Instead the King of England controlled the Church of Scotland and episcopacy was the medium by which he did. It is hard to see why the Scottish Episcopal Church should resent being called 'The English Kirk'. In the early seventeenth century an episcopal church in Scotland was simply the natural way in which the King of England imposed his will in ecclesiastical matters. It is true that the bishops were Scotsmen. But then the English King because of his own immense reservoir of power was able to offer power to Scottish divines. It was different from the prophetic power which the Kirk of Knox and Melville claimed. Instead it was hierarchical power, power over the clergy. And as anyone who offers power to the ministry (or indeed to any other profession) will find takers, James and Charles got their bishops. If the latter had any qualms about acting as instruments for a man who though nominally King of Scotland was actually using the considerable power of England to control its northern neighbour, they had precedent for their action in the disloyalty syndrome which we have noted as a factor in Scottish affairs. And Scottish bishops in addition had received from the English ones the apostolic succession. The value of this curious piece of quasi-theology is that it is a device which enables those who hold the succession to persuade the credulous and indeed themselves that their will is the will of God. In this case the will was the will of the King of England and it suited the latter extremely well to spread the idea that he who opposed him was opposed to God.

Revolt, when it came, seems to have been a result of Charles I overplaying his hand. Not content like his father with a Church of Scotland amenable to the will of the King of England, he determined to have one reconstituted from head to foot on the English model of Laud's canons. These, which precipitated the crisis were for the most part a transcript of the English canons of 1604. The remnants of conciliar government were swept away from the Church of Scotland and canons which had been framed for a different church in a different situation in a different country were imposed on it by an English archbishop backed by his royal master. Now in the terms of the dogma of the one church, there is perhaps nothing wrong with this. This only goes to show the fatuous nature of that dogma. For in practice no country in which there is a vestige of nationalism will allow one of its basic institutions, the Church or any other, to be reconstituted by the Diktat of a foreigner. It is hard to imagine Englishmen to-day allowing their public schools to be transformed into co-educational high schools as the result of the decree of an American. And Englishmen of the seventeenth century were no less nationalistic. When the Scots moved by the same dogma of the One Church tried to impose their ecclesiastical constitution on the English they were soon taught the folly of their ways. But that is to anticipate.

For the present it is sufficient to note that in these circumstances Charles I and Laud succeeded in uniting Scotland as no one else had done. The bishops of course supported the English Archbishop and King. From the Edinburgh mob up every other group revolted against the Archbishop of Canterbury's *Gleichschaltung* of the Scottish Church. The four emergency committees set up to organise the opposition bore testimony to its widespread nature. One committee or 'Table' was that of the

burgesses, another that of the country gentlemen, a third that of
the ministers, and the fourth, that of our old friends, the nobles.
The protest in which the opposition found expression was
ratified by these four committees. It is the document known as
the National Covenant of 1637.

The word 'covenanter' has become emotionally charged in
Scotland and for that reason it is best to try and discuss the
National Covenant as dispassionately as possible. As a religious
document it is not particularly inspiring. There are some
tactical reasons for this. It was thought advisable to make its
first part a reiteration of the Negative Confession of 1581 which
King James VI had drawn up and himself signed. As its name
denotes this was a fairly negative rejection of Roman Catholicism. Its most interesting feature is a condemnation of the Pope
for his 'cruelty to the innocent divorced'. This was making use
of the late King to reply to the alleged Romanising tendencies
of Laud's canons and Liturgy. The second part of the National
Covenant was a judicious citation of the various acts of parliament setting up Presbyterianism. This was a valid enough
demonstration of the unconstitutional nature of Laud's
measures. In the third part comes the actual bond or covenant
whereby the signatories bind themselves to maintain the above
Protestant and Presbyterian religion. They also pledged themselves that 'we shall to the uttermost of our power, with our
means and lives, stand to the defence of our dread Soveraigne,
The Kings Majesty, his Person and Authority, in the defence of
the foresaid true Religion, Liberties and Lawes of the King-
dome'. This second pledge might have tactical value as a
counter to the charge of treason, what the covenant calls 'the
foul aspersions of rebellion, combination, or what elses our
adversaries from their craft and malice would put upon us'.
In actual fact the covenanters were combining. For earlier
in the Covenant they had declared 'So that whatever shall be
done to the least of us for that cause, shall be taken as done to us
all in general and to everyone of us in particular'. It would have
been well if they had stated with equal frankness that they were
prepared to resist by force any attempt of the King to over-
throw the construction of their national church. They were in

fact prepared to do this and if they had not been, their covenant would have been useless. The pledge to defend the authority of the King was in fact incompatible with the pledge to maintain the Presbyterian form of religion, for Episcopacy was the religion which served the King's power interests. The juxtaposition of the two pledges in the Covenant proved fateful and in the end fatal to the covenanters.

There was some opposition to the covenant—particularly in the other university towns. But it united Scotsmen as they have seldom been united before or since. They were united, Professor Watt tells us, on the basis of religious conviction, nationalism and self-interest, a formidable combination of motives. Just how formidable it was, the Marquess of Hamilton, the King's Commissioner in Scotland, was to find as soon as he crossed the border. The Hamilton gentlemen, the cadets of his own great family did not ride to meet him. The new spirit in the country was greater than the ancient Scottish custom of family loyalty which had once bound even a Knox and a Bothwell together.

In the show down that was bound to follow, the Scots had what for them were two quite unusual advantages over the English. The first was in the military field. They had the advantage of what we would call an excellent pool of officer material in the Scots who had fought in Germany. It was the Thirty Years War veterans, from the Swedish general Leslie downwards who made the covenanting force into perhaps the best army Scotland has ever possessed. It was not very difficult for it to seize Newcastle and cut off London's coal supplies, and so apply economic sanctions.

Then for once it was England and not Scotland which was divided. On the eve of the English Civil War the London Parliament was not likely to provide the King with funds to fight the Scots. And once that war broke out both sides were likely to find in the Scots army a desirable ally.

So that in the late 1630's the power equations were yielding unexpected results. For once a united and militarily superior Scotland faced a disunited and militarily inferior England. At last, the Scots could negotiate from strength. Within a few years this promising situation had ended in utter disaster. A fine and skilfully led army had been irretrievably defeated in the field, its survivors had been left to drag out their existence as prisoners-of-war in the Belsen-like hell of Durham Cathedral and a hitherto unconquered country was occupied by a foreign army.

There is no doubt who was responsible for this catastrophe. It was the Church of Scotland. Or to be precise it was the work of a perennial element which has been that Church's greatest liability, the will of God men, the High-Flying Party, or as David Hume once called them 'the furious Christians'. Canonizing their own limited insights as the will of God, these divines are thus set free to enjoy the pleasures of unlimited denunciation of all who disagree with them. For are the latter not by definition enemies of God and Christ? This combination of theocentricity and denunciation is a device whereby we make use of God to enable us to dislike our fellow men more violently. It is by no means a spent force. Even to-day for a General Assembly speaker to refer to a course of action as the will of Christ means only too often that he is about to give a brother Christian hell for opposing it.

But we must not pass to modern times before we have examined more closely this, the most spectacular of all the disasters produced by the will of God party in the Church of Scotland.

The churchmen who brought Scotland to its hitherto lowest ebb in the 1640's were committed to two convictions about the Will of God. First—and this gives them a curiously topical air— they were convinced that it was God's will that there should be one church with a single ecclesiastical structure for Scotland, England and Ireland. Anything else was sin and had to be abolished.

'We . . . shall endeavour to bring the Churches of God in the three Kingdoms, to the nearest conjunction and uniformity in Religion, Confession of Faith, Form of Church-Government, Directory for Worship and Catechising . . .

'We shall in like manner, without respect of persons, endeavour the Extirpation of Popery, Prelacy (that is, Church-government by Archbishops, Bishops . . . and all other ecclesiastical officers depending on that Hierarchy) Superstition, Heresy, Schism, Prophanesse, and whatsoever shall be found contrary to sound Doctrine and the power of Godliness . . . that the Lord may be one and His Name one in the three Kingdoms.'

As unable as any modern Ecumenical to see church government as a product of national tradition and power structure, they were committed to an ecclesiastical imperialism. Having just rejected the Anglican archbishop's attempt to reconstitute their Church on English lines they made an ecclesiastical reconstruction of England on Scottish lines, a condition of the entry of their army into the English Civil War on the parliamentary side. The attempt was not quite so hopeless as it seems, for in the City of London and in Parliament there was a strong indigenous English Presbyterian nucleus. But in the main the efforts of the Scots Commissioners at the Westminster Assembly to make the Church of England Presbyterian depended on the achievements of the Scots army in England. The presence of foreign troops on English soil while necessary in times of weakness is never however entirely congenial to English nationalists —even today their German allies find themselves firing their rockets in the Outer Hebrides and their American ones have to manoeuvre their Polaris submarines in the Firth of Clyde. When through the development of Cromwell's largely Congregationalist and sectarian army, the Scottish troops became redundant, the project for making England Presbyterian was over.

The closing of this curious chapter in Scottish ecclesiastical imperialism would not in itself have been disastrous were it not for another key concept which we have already noticed at work in Scottish history, namely the Old Testament blueprint. The belief that the Kingdoms of Judah and Israel at their purest form a pattern to which it is God's will that Scotland should conform is already present in Knox's famous remark 'I have read that Ahab was ane King and Jezebel was ane Queen'. It is expressed even to-day in a lingering sabbatarianism and a national distaste for mackerel. But it is in the middle seventeenth century that the belief proved most disastrous and we must examine the various forms which it took.

First and ugliest it took the form of giving no quarter to prisoners-of-war. The Old Testament blueprint meant that officers who sought to spare their prisoners-of-war were liable to receive from the ministers the rebuke handed out to Saul in I Sam. 15 for exercising a like clemency. There is evidence, for instance, that the Covenanting commander would have spared the garrison at Dunaverty. It was his chaplain who insisted on having them massacred.

On another plane, the Old Testament blueprint for Scotland kept the Scots from the republicanism which was the obvious solution to their problem and which would have cut through the ambiguities of the National Covenant that we have noted above. But republicanism is a classical not an Old Testament concept (though some hard things are said of Kings in 1 Sam. 8). The result was that the Scots were committed to the futility of their dealings with the young Charles II. They crowned a King and then insulted him. They supported monarchy on conditions that no seventeenth-century monarch would accept.

If the Old Testament blueprint for Scotland ruled out republicanism, it closed the door just as firmly on toleration. The latter was not an attitude much favoured by the more denunciatory prophetic figures of the Old Testament. In these the Scots divines saw their prototypes. Hence the idea of toleration in the middle seventeenth century found a lodging not in the Scots army but in the English Parliamentary one. Cynics may say that it did so because of the presence in that army of the English independents who could not hope for dominance and so opted for the next best thing. But it is fair to point out their advocacy of toleration also followed from their separation of church and state, a separation unheard of in the Old Testament and hence unacceptable in mid-seventeenth century Scotland. In this the seventeenth-century Scots were definitely not forward looking, for toleration and republicanism were to be the principles on which a new and greater England was to rise beyond the western seas. And although tolerance or, to give it its proper title, spiritual freedom, is threatened again, it is being championed to-day by the more liberal against the more reactionary elements in the Roman Catholics. Here we can see one bright feature in inter-church relations to offset the ever-growing threat of Anglican imperialism.

There is one final and quite fateful consequence of the acceptance of the Old Testament as a blueprint for Scotland. The Old Testament is the story of a nation which ceased to be a nation and became a church. It is hardly surprising if Scotland, having taken the Old Testament as a political handbook, has met with a like fate. In the mid-seventeenth century the Scots followed the Old Testament to the extent of transposing political and national realities into an ecclesiastical key. The English rebels asked for a league between the two countries, the ensuring compromise being a Solemn League and Covenant.[1] It was an alliance between a nation and a church for what the English wanted most was an army and what the Scots wanted most was, they called in Old Testament fashion, suppression of idolatry and the establishment of the One Church in the two kingdoms. In the end, of course, English nationalism was so strong as to make Englishmen dislike both a Scottish army and a Scottish inspired church settlement. Mr. A. S. P. Woodhouse talks of the odium of a Scottish army on English soil. English nationalism is a very strong force indeed and the odium can still be detected in the words in which a highly esteemed English writer of our century describes ' . . . the system of church government which the supercilious Scotch Commissioners at the Westminster Assembly steered to inconclusive victory . . . "Mr. Henderson", wrote the insufferable Baillie, "has ready now a short treatise, much called for, of our church discipline". In June 1646 an unenthusiastic Parliament accepted the ordinance which after a three years debate of intolerable tedium, emerged from the Assembly's Committee on the Discipline and Government of the church.'[2]

One must not exaggerate the difference between the two countries in the seventeenth century. The Civil War period was one of religious crisis for many Englishmen. And even Mr. Tawney's bete-noir, Baillie, had more insight into the way

1. I owe this point and the one made below to my friend the Rev. Frank Gibson.

2. Tawney, *Religion and the Rise of Capitalism.*

power factors affect church government than have the Ecumenicals to-day.[1] But by and large the contrast remains. Acceptance
of an Old Testament blueprint for Scotland led the Scots to
transpose national factors on to the ecclesiastical key. Such a
procedure even the English Puritans with their separation of the
realms of nature and grace were able to avoid. The difference,
as we shall see, has proved a fateful one.

---

1. I am indebted to Mr. Gibson (see p. 78) for the following delightful
extract from Baillie's letters. Re Parliament not deciding Government of
Church. 'The Assembly has plied them with petition upon petition, the City
also, both ministers and magistrates; but all in vain—Had our army been but
one 15,000 men in England, our advice would have been followed quickly in
all things; but our lamentable posture at home and our weakness here, makes
our desires contemptible—In this case our last refuge is to God, and under
Him to the City.' (To Mr. Robert Ramsay 15.1.46.) 'with which, we propose
not to meddle in haste, until, it pleases God to advance our Army, which we
expect will much assist our arguments.' (1648 G. Gillespie. Vol. 1. liv.)

11

1707

I T is almost impossible to explain to Englishmen why Scotsmen did what they did in 1707. For in that year they did what no responsible Englishman, however restrained his nationalism, would even dream of doing without any federal safeguards. They committed the representatives of their country to being a permanent minority in the Parliament of a foreign country. Can anyone for a moment imagine the English putting their affairs under a permanent majority of Frenchmen and Germans? The actual circumstances of the negotiation of the Treaty of Union are even more incredible. The Scottish Parliament actually allowed its Union Commissioners to be chosen by the Queen, knowing full well that the monarch's choice would be influenced by her English advisers. Can anyone imagine the English Parliament allowing itself to be represented at the Brussels negotiations not by Mr. Heath but by some English nominee of Dr. Adenauer and General de Gaulle? If they had, history would certainly have been different, but the supposition is so wild as not to be worth entertaining.

What Scotsmen did in 1707 is the kind of action inconceivable for not only England but for India and Pakistan and for all the new African states so dear to the Kirk's Foreign Mission Committee. Yet it would be very hard to find a Scottish history book which condemns it. One does not require to be much of a psychologist to see here the seeds of the Scottish neurosis. The Scotsman is conditioned to admire in his own countrymen the kind of action which he and everyone else is expected to despise in an Englishman. From this initial factor come the other neurotic aspects of the modern Scottish viewpoint, the sahib-sepoy view of Anglo-Scottish relations, the view quite unproved but widely accepted axiomatically by upper-middle class Scotsmen that English institutions are U and Scottish institutions non-U, and the conception of Scotland's destiny as that of an ultimate Poona which is still widely held in the Highlands and the non-urban parts of the Borders. These view points are so alien to the attitudes, e.g. of Icelanders or Norwegians that they can only be ascribed to the pathology of Scotland. Only in the light of these neurotic symptoms can a document like the Bishops' Report be understood. And perhaps most of them go back to the compulsion to approve the quite un-English action of the Scotsmen of 1707.

About the actual happenings of 1707 not much need be said. Since the reign of William and Mary the Scots Parliament had become something like an effective force. Its Act of Security in 1704 even without Fletcher of Saltoun's republican limitations meant that Scotland was no longer a pawn to be managed from London. The English Parliament's Alien Act of 1705 replied to this challenge to its imperialism by a threat to Scottish trade. The situation was obviously one of crisis, heightened by the background of a Catholic Jacobite claim to the throne of both countries. Why the crisis should have been resolved by a final and permanent Scottish surrender is the almost insoluble question. Bribery may supply part of the answer but the verdict of responsible historians is that on this occasion it was hardly more than routine. Materialism may supply another part of the answer. Scotland was a poor country and the merchant class may have been ready to trade their birthright for a mess of pottage in the shape of access to the English colonies. If they had waited just seventy years until the Boston Tea Party they would have got a good deal of pottage free.

Bribery and materialism no doubt played their part but something like the disloyalty or treason syndrome must be postulated to account for those who held power in Scotland acting in the way they did in defiance of impotent national feeling. Since the Reformation and indeed for long before it, treason had been a live option for the Scottish power operator in a way it had not been for his English counterpart. Treason is in fact the correlate of anarchy with its inevitable lack of a centre for loyalty. A country can tolerate a little treason but with too much it ceases to be a country. At the Reformation, Bothwell, the figure untouched by treason in his country, was a discredited minority of one and a Scotland whose leading figures were a Knox, a Maitland, a Moray and a Mary Stuart was left to face an England whose nationalism was expressed in Shakespeare's words . . .

> 'This royal throne of kings, this sceptr'd isle,
> This earth of majesty, this seat of Mars,
> This other Eden, demi-paradise,
> This fortress built by Nature for herself
> Against infection and the hand of war,
> This happy breed of men, this little world,
> This precious stone set in the silver sea,
> Which serves it in the office of a wall,
> Or as a moat defensive to a house,
> Against the envy of less happier lands;
> This blessed plot, this earth, this realm, this England.'

And in these first years of the eighteenth century Scotland, in the hands of men content to leave the final negotiations for their country in the hands of those of their number whom it suited the English to appoint, had to face an England raised to nationalist ecstasy by the victories of Marlborough. To such confrontations there could only be one end.

If the disloyalty syndrome can be observed in the events leading to 1707 so can that complementary factor in Scottish history, the Old Testament blueprint. The historians agree that the Church of Scotland could have prevented the Union of 1707. The Church of Scotland was in fact torn in two in its attitude to the union of 1707. On the one hand there was its fear of a successful invasion of Scotland by Catholic Jacobitism. Union with England was a safeguard against such a contingency. On the other hand the English Act against occasional conformity which disqualified non-members of the Church of England from public office made it abundantly clear that there was not going to be much future for members of the Church of Scotland in England. The Church of Scotland, all agree, could have stopped the Union and did not. For this the ultimate reason must lie in something deeper than an estimate of the possible political and religious contingencies of the moment. A step so drastic and so irrevocable as consent to union could only be taken by those convinced that Israel could cease to be a nation and still remain as a church. In spite of the eighteenth century the Old Testament was still operative as a blueprint for Scotland. Hence it was that the union legislation which contains none of the federal provisions so essential in a union between two states, has massive safeguards for the church. Its Presbyterian constitution is guaranteed for all time thenceforward. Clearly any attempt now or at anytime to set up bishops in the Church of Scotland is a breach of the Treaty of Union between England and Scotland.

Whether the guarantees are worth much is a point that depends on whether there is such a thing as English constitutional law or whether, on the contrary, the sovereignty of parliament means that any English parliament can undo any legislation passed by one of its predecessors. That is the key question. For the assumption that in 1707 England ceased to exist and that a new country, Great Britain, whose constitution was the Act of Union, came into being is, of course, completely unacceptable to English nationalism. If any Scots have been silly enough to think otherwise it is only because their own disloyalty syndrome has made it impossible for them to understand the intense nationalism of Englishmen.

Just how little weight could be put on the ecclesiastical guarantees written into the Act of Union was made clear to the Church of Scotland as early as 1712. In that year the London Parliament in defiance of the Act of Union introduced patronage into the Church of Scotland. This action was the direct cause of the divisions which bedevilled the Church of Scotland up to the reunion of 1929, and particularly of the Disruption of 1843, which rendered the Church of Scotland largely impotent before the problems thrown up by the Industrial Revolution. It is important to be clear on this point for there is an occasional hint on the part of the Anglican Ecumenicals[1] that these divisions were brought about by the inherently fissiparous tendency of a non-episcopal Scottish church. Their originating cause lies, on the contrary, in the Act of 1712, an act in which English M.P.'s secure in their overwhelming majority in the London parliament broke a treaty which their country had made with a weaker neighbour a few years earlier. None of us who, even in this generation, have had the wearing task of trying to get Free Church ideas into line with the realities of the post-1929 Church of Scotland will be inclined either to underestimate or to bless the 1712 breach of the Treaty of Union.

We have seen that the failure of the Church of Scotland leaders to prevent the union could only have its foundation in the deep conviction that Israel the church could survive the disappearance of Israel the nation. And in fact the effort of their action has been to condemn their countrymen to a position like that of Jews in pre-1914 Vienna, that of second-class citizens. You can only deny that position if you maintain that on this island a man who has been educated at an ancient Scottish school and an ancient Scottish university has an equal chance of reaching high position as a man educated at an ancient English school and an ancient English university. And nobody is going to maintain that.

As it happened this consequence was averted for some time after the union by the simple fact noted by Halevy, that Scots M.P.'s in London sold their votes to whatever government was in power. In return they received so many places in the armed forces and the public services. Given the 1707 union with its complete lack of Federal provisions, e.g. such as senatorial nomination to West Point, the arrangement had something to be said for it and its termination does not seem to have brought many advantages to either Scotland or England. Maclean and Burgess are hardly an improvement on David Hume in the Paris Embassy and Sir John Moore and the other Scottish peninsular war generals compare not unfavourably with the generals of an English tradition who were in control of the British Army in 1914 and 1939.

1. e.g. by John Lawrence in *The Hard Facts of Unity*.

With the Reform Act this mutually advantageous traffic in votes and posts ceased with disastrous results for Scotland. The nationalism of the English was such that when they were no longer compelled to receive Scotsmen in the public services they ceased to do so. In the figures for the 1965 Method I entry into the Administrative Home and Diplomatic Services of the 32 successful places, 30 went to graduates of English universities, one to an Irish and one to a Scottish graduate. These figures are the more interesting in that Scottish universities unlike Oxford and Cambridge (26 of the 32 places) insist that their modern languages students live in the countries whose languages they profess, a valuable safeguard against insular outlook for future members of the diplomatic service—assuming, of course, such a safeguard is desired.

One should not, of course, make too much of these 1965 figures. For one thing England has ceased to be a great power. A place in her diplomatic service is no longer all that much of a prize. For another, intelligent Scotsmen, like intelligent Jews in pre-1914 Austria, have learned to be content to be siphoned from the professions barred to them into those where barriers are much more difficult to erect. In medicine and engineering success goes with the possession of certain skills. It is hard for nationalist barriers to be placed against those who possess these skills. It is therefore understandable why medicine and engineering should be the two professions with which Scotsmen should be most closely associated.

The other alternative is deracination. This is always an alternative in a situation dominated by racialism, whether the racial prejudice be imposed on the coloured, the Jew or the Scot. The Cape coloured girl can have her hair straightened in the attempt to 'pass' as a white South African. The Viennese Jew could become baptised in order to 'pass' as an Austrian fit for Kaiserliche and Königliche service. In the same way a Scotsman can become confirmed at an English public school and go on to Oxford in an attempt to 'pass' as an Englishman. To do so is virtually essential if the Scotsman wishes a diplomatic career. It is nearly as essential if he wishes a certain kind of political career. Recent figures quoted in The Glasgow Herald of

November 23rd 1965 show that of 23 Scottish Conservative M.P.'s 18 were educated at an English school or university. It is very hard to imagine English Conservatives accepting a similar situation. And indeed Scotland is the only small nation in Europe which submits to the humiliation of having its diplomats and legislators conditioned to behaviour patterns other than its own.

Deracination is widely practised but never talked about in Scotland to-day. It is a fascinating phenomenon which we must discuss at length in a future chapter. Only in the light of it is the nature of the Ecumenical Movement in Scotland intelligible.

The Church of Scotland as at present constituted is undeeracinated. No post in it is closed to the products of Scottish, German or American, or for that matter, English universities. The Scottish Episcopal Church is, of course, deracinated. All its leading figures are the products of English schools and universities. For the Church of Scotland with its million odd members to submit to the terms of the Scottish Episcopal Church with its 56,000 members is what the Ecumenical Party in the Church of Scotland wish. It is a desire for a diplomatic surrender so incredible that it can only be understood in terms of racialism. Only to one who holds the sahib-sepoy view of Anglo-Scottish relations and the view that Scottish institutions are non-U and English ones U does the proposition make sense.

For the present let us try and draw up something like a fair balance sheet on the union. Here again we get the fairest and clearest results if we go to the power equations. Scotland never was and never could be a great power. England was once such a power. E. H. Carr in his writings has made it abundantly clear how vast is the difference between a great power and a small power, a fact of which Englishmen since 1945 have slowly, gradually and painfully become aware. Those individual Scotsmen who by the methods indicated earlier in this chapter gained some share in directing the destinies of pre-1945 England attained a degree of power which would never have been theirs if Scotland had remained independent. Even the jackal's share of a great power is not inconsiderable. On the other hand it is impossible to look at the list of names on a World War I memorial in a Scottish village without feeling that as a result of the Union large numbers of Scotsmen met premature, unnecessary and irrelevant deaths. And one has only to contrast the economic state of the Highlands with North Norway or that of Shetland with Faroe to see the economic price that has been paid for union.

One other favourable aspect of the union must be mentioned. The idea of the Kingdoms of England and Scotland ceasing to exist in 1707 and being succeeded by a new and united kingdom has always been intolerable to English nationalism. At best it has been a pathetic illusion existing in the fantasies of some Scotsmen. But the idea of a United Kingdom has at least one merit. It is the idea of a Kingdom which has two churches, the Church of England and the Church of Scotland, each with its own separate constitution. By 1707 western man was beginning to emancipate himself from the horrors of the idea of the One Church which had bespattered Europe with the blood of the seventeenth century religious wars. Whatever the faults of the Treaty of Union, it is at least a witness to the emergence of the new and cleaner idea of denominationalism.

It is, of course, this aspect of the Treaty of Union which annoys the pro-Anglican ecumenical party in the Church of Scotland. By one of the pleasant ironies of history the supreme achievement of Scottish anti-nationalism has become a major stumbling block to the Scottish anti-nationalists of to-day. The latter have one criticism to make of their eighteenth century predecessors. Their surrender was not unconditional enough.

12

Coexistence and Disruption

At the beginning of the nineteenth century ecclesiastical relations between Scotland and England were remarkably good. The eighteenth century and the Aufklärung had done their work and in the main it was a very good work. Reasonableness and tolerance prevailed. David Hume might still be molested on occasion by those whom he termed 'furious Christians' but he was on excellent terms with the moderates of the Church of Scotland and chose Edinburgh as the place of his retirement. This sensible spirit began to initiate a new happy period of coexistence between the two national churches. Even the arch-English nationalist, Dr. Johnson, could find little to blame in an Island minister who could talk with him of Leibniz and Bayle. And when Thomas Chalmers, then the leading ornament of the Scottish pulpit was called to London to give the fashionable Christian Influence Society lectures, he chose to devote them to a defence of the established Church of England.

The refreshingly sober tone of early nineteenth century ecclesiastical thought is shown in the work of Chalmers (1780–1847). In his time one main difference between England and Scotland lay in the Poor Law arrangements. In England these were secular in character and the money necessary for the Poor relief was raised by compulsory assessment. In Scotland they were ecclesiastical and voluntary. The money necessary for poor relief came from the offertory plate of the parish church (minister's stipend and upkeep of church and manse being a burden on the landed proprietors of the parish). It is easy to see the strain that the Industrial Revolution placed on the Scottish system of poor relief. The population of a hitherto rural parish would be increased by the erection of a factory. But the factory might be in a part of the parish remote from the church so that its erection would not mean increased church attendance or increased church collection. Then in some trade depression the the factory would close down. The Kirk Session would be left to meet a vastly increased parish destitution with more or less the pre-Industrial Revolution church collections. It was no wonder that in the South of Scotland parishes were going over to the English system of compulsory assessment.

With this trend towards the English system, Chalmers had no sympathy. He proposed to meet the economic crisis of the Industrial Revolution by the church, at the centre of every parish inculcating the traditional virtues of the Scottish way of life. Believing as he did that wages were inevitably fixed by the law of supply and demand, he wanted the working man to enter that market on the best possible terms. He wanted, in fact, a seller's market in labour, the job chasing the man rather than the man chasing the job. 'We should regard it as a far more healthful state of the community, if our workmen, instead of having to seek employment, were to be sought after'. This healthy state of affairs was to be brought about primarily by seeing that labour had a scarcity value and was therefore highly paid. Hence Chalmers advocated late marriage, he extolled the old Scottish custom of delaying marriage until there was a full plenishing—hire purchase would have been anathema to him. One of the functions of the church, and one of its ways in which it could promote a healthy economy was by inculcating the sexual continence which the discipline of late marriage entailed. The employee's bargaining position over against that of the employer was to be further strengthened by the workman accumulating savings, so that he wasn't so desperate for work as to have to accept the first offer made to him by an employer, however inadequate the remuneration. 'The simple ability of the workman to maintain himself for so many weeks without his accustomed wages, is that which brings up these wages, in a far shorter period than they otherwise would, to their customary level'.

The limitations of Chalmers' social and economic teaching are obvious. He was over optimistic in that he considered that moral factors by themselves could deal with economic crises of unemployment. His devotion to his own ideals and to what he considered to be the traditional Scottish way of life kept him from seeing the real misery in the industrialised Lowlands and in the impoverished Highlands. But in this context we are concerned simply with Chalmers' view of the church. In refreshing contrast to that of many ecclesiastics his conception of the church is empirical, functioning and non-nutty. He really did try to see the church not in the light of what it claimed to be but in the light of what it actually was and actually did. By so doing he emancipated himself from the fantasy world in which the power claims of ecclesiastics are taken seriously because God has been called in and made use of to bolster them up. For this kind of ecclesiastical ideology he had no use whatever. It is entirely understandable that he pained Mr. Gladstone by his indifference to the doctrine of apostolic succession. In this and in other matters he would equally have pained the contemporary Ecumenical movement. Thus the present Ecumenical treatment of the eldership is a pretty transparent attempt to facilitate an Anglican take-over bid by downgrading the eldership. This is done by having recourse to one sided New Testament exegesis—a shrewd choice of field for the power struggle between cleric and elder. The latter feels himself at a disadvantage in the technicalities of what purports to be interpretation of the Greek New Testament. The next step is to seize on New Testament passages which suggest that the elder is really a deacon and further New Testament passages which suggest that deacons have to do what bishops tell them. If other contrary New Testament passages are conveniently ignored another nail is hammered into the coffin of non-episcopal churches.

Chalmers' treatment of the eldership on the other hand was quite different. He was concerned much more simply with what elders actually were in Scotland and what function they could perform for, as he put it, the Christian good of Scotland, in the social and economic conditions. These two treatments of the eldership, that of the Ecumenicals and that of Chalmers can be taken as exemplifying two different conceptions of the theology of the church. On the former, the Ecumenical view, the theology of the church is a power struggle carried on under the cover of what purports to be New Testament interpretation. On Chalmers' view, the theology of the church is a field where the theologian can talk openly and dispassionately with the sociologist and the psychiatrist and where he does not try to absolutise any ecclesiastical power structure by saying that those who oppose it, oppose God. I would say that it is the former not the latter conception of the theology of the church which is calculated to bring a blush to the cheek of the theologian. And I would say that it is the latter which is suited to the twentieth century.

Chalmers' attitude to England is equally commendable. He very properly was a profound admirer of the country and of its institutions and particularly of the Church of England. This did not mean that he had the slightest desire to copy these institutions. He shared the view of such wise Englishmen as Edmund Burke and in our own day, Sir Arthur Bryant,[1] that a country's institutions are an organic growth capable of development but not necessarily of transplanting or of having an alien pattern imposed upon them. It is impossible to imagine him signing either the Solemn League and Covenant or The Bishops Report. He was in this as in some other respects a pre-eminently sensible man.

In the life of Chalmers, however, the good sense of Chalmers' basic position did not prevail and tragedy supervened. This tragedy is part of the tragedy of Scotland and we must therefore see how it took shape. We have seen that for Chalmers the church had an indispensable role to play in the social and economic structure of Scotland. But in order to perform this role, it had to be flexible particularly in the changing conditions of the Industrial Revolution. Chalmers did his best to secure that flexibility. To cope with the situation where a factory grew up remote from the parish church, he embarked on a programme of church extension to meet the needs of the

1. It is significant that Sir Arthur Bryant, who visited the General Assembly of the Church of Scotland at the time of the Bishops Report, declared himself opposed to that document.

new industrial population. The London government refused him the money for his new churches—according to a letter which W. E. Gladstone sent him, largely because of the opposition of English free church M.P.'s. Undeterred, Chalmers set about raising it himself. Being that unusual combination, both a first class orator and a first class organiser, he succeeded and built his new churches. But he was only to receive a further setback. The Scottish Courts ruled that the ministers of his new churches were ineligible for a seat in presbytery. In his efforts to make the church more flexible and so more able to serve the community both spiritually and, as he thought, in the economic field, the civil authorities, both executive and judicial, had impeded him at every turn.

Legislative action to make the Scottish parochial system less rigid could have saved the situation. Had there been a parliament in Edinburgh no doubt such action would have been forthcoming. A London parliament had other things to do. To be fair to it, Chalmers, the possessor of an irascible nature which his religious conversion never enabled him to remedy, simply lacked the capacity for patient political negotiation. The orator and organiser was no diplomat.

In the circumstances tragedy was perhaps inevitable, and here we can only briefly trace its course. Ever since his conversion as a young minister, Chalmers had been a member of the Evangelical Party of the Church of Scotland. In itself there could seem little wrong with this. In the eighteenth century the Church of Scotland had flourished quite well on a two party system of Evangelical and Moderate. The main political aim of the Evangelical Party was the laudable one of somehow setting aside the 1712 breach of the Treaty of Union. In 1833 they seem to have achieved that by an Act of the General Assembly. This act, the Veto Act, circumvented the patronage imposed in London in 1712 to the extent that it laid down that in a church vacancy the patron's nominee could be set aside if the majority of the male heads of families in the parish vetoed him. In fairness to the Evangelical party it must be said that they did not consider they were acting illegally in passing this Act of Assembly. They had excellent legal opinion and in the Assembly a Lord of Session seconded the Act. Notwithstanding, the civil courts later ruled that in passing the Veto Act the Assembly had acted *ultra vires*.

In the ensuing crisis the only sensible thing would have been for the next Assembly to have repealed the Veto Act and to have sought legislation abolishing patronage in the London Parliament. Attempts were in fact made to do this but they came to nothing. And in the meantime the Evangelical Party had taken the bit between its teeth and used its majority in the Assembly to retain the Veto Act. The result was ecclesiastical chaos. For in a disputed vacancy presbyteries now had to decide whether to apply the Veto Act in which case they were liable to be imprisoned for breaking the law of the land or not to apply it, in which case they were liable to be deposed from office for not obeying their ecclesiastical superiors. Auchterarder took the former course and its members were reprimanded but not imprisoned by the civil court. Marnoch took the latter and its ministerial members were deposed from the ministry by the ecclesiastical one. The end to an impossible situation came in 1843 when the Church of Scotland split in two.

The result was tragedy for the country and—though he never admitted it—for Chalmers. The ten years struggle which led to the Disruption had taken the church's eye off the ball—the ball being, as Chalmers had seen from his early years, the Industrial Revolution and its impact on the social life of Scotland. After the Disruption the church could not take what Chalmers conceived to be its place in the social and economic functioning of Scotland. In consequence the English Poor Law System, anathema to Chalmers, had to be introduced into Scotland. And the consequence of that, as one of his Highland correspondents was to point out to Chalmers, was that the Highland landlords, for the first time legally responsible for the relief of their destitute tenancy, now had an excellent motive for embarking the latter on emigrant ships on the waters of the Atlantic.

Why then did Chalmers play the part he did in bringing about the Disruption? Perhaps the secret lies in those who were his chief lieutenants in the Evangelical Party, Candlish and

Cunningham. Younger than Chalmers they were even more irascible. Indeed the reader of their biographies is left with the impression that the career of each of them was simply a procession from one ecclesiastical brawl to another. After the Disruption, which they jointly engineered, they fell out and never spoke to one another for ten years. Unlike Chalmers who would have been famous if there had never been a Disruption, they had no feeling for the immense social and economic issues which caused untold misery both in the Industrial Lowlands and in the Highlands.

Why did Chalmers play the part he did in making his own ideal for Scotland impossible? Part of the explanation lies in the nature of the ecclesiastical politics into which he was drawn. The ecclesiastical party to which he belonged had a perfectly legitimate and indeed laudable central political object, the abolition of the 1712 breach of the Act of Union. But in order to gain its ends it transposed its activities into a theocentric key. By taking to itself the great name of the Evangel and not some colourless designation like that of the Moderates, its rival party, it successfully conveyed the idea that to oppose it was to oppose the Gospel. By the third decade of the nineteenth century some of the leading members were tinged with the Romanticism of the period. They like to imagine themselves as akin to the covenanters, ignoring the fact that the government of Lord Melbourne, whatever its demerits, was very unlike that of Archbishop Laud. They used accordingly to boast that like the covenanters they feared not the face of man. This they took to imply that they feared God. In practice it only meant that they went around being very rude to everyone who disagreed with them. And once the Evangelicals gained a majority in the General Assembly, they accused anyone who opposed their party measures of infringing the Crown Rights of the Redeemer.

The will of God was thus once again in the saddle of the Church of Scotland. And as in the 1640's the result was disaster, a church impotent in the face of the appalling problems caused by the Lowland Industrial Revolution and the collapse of the Highland civilisation. That the disaster was inevitable is not hard to see. To enthrone the will of God in ecclesiastical party politics is to drive out love. For the point in calling your party policy the will of God is just that it enables you to give hell to the man who opposes it. For does that not make him the enemy of God? And what a wonderful opportunity to enable you Christian that you are, to give vent to all the lovelessness in your nature.

Anyone who doubts this should study the lives of Chalmer's lieutenants in the Disruption struggle, Candlish and Cunningham. Vastly inferior to Chalmers in greatness, they surpassed him in irascibility. They did not hesitate from the really dreadful step of deposing from the Christian ministry the Marnoch ministers who conscientiously disagreed with them.

The moral of the Disruption struggle is clear enough to see. First, and in the local setting, any ecclesiastical party which identifies its policy with the will of God has got a hold of the right formula for breaking the Church of Scotland. For it is a formula which precludes discussion and makes possible lovelessness and even prayer against one's brother in Christ. Secondly, and on a much wider scale, ecclesiastical movements can only be properly understood if they are transposed out of the theocentric key. This is not an easy thing to ask for. It means asking ecclesiastics to admit that they like power and on occasion make use of God to get more power. It is costing to admit this, much more costing than just talking about the sin of disunion.

But this is the only way if there is to be understanding of ecclesiastical movements. The Disruption, with which we have dealt very briefly, is an important ecclesiastical event. But we only begin to understand it if we transpose it out of the theocentric key. The will of God does not help us to understand why the Highlanders disrupted almost to a man. The fact that the policy of the Moderate party coincided with the will of the Highland landlords in an era of clearance and eviction does.

In 1816, Patrick Sellar, factor to the Duchess of Sutherland, had been tried before Lord Pitmilly at Inverness on charges, one of which was wilful fire-raising, attended with the most aggravated circumstances of cruelty, if not murder. It was not denied that Sellar had put a woman of ninety-two out of her house into a byre with a leaking roof and no door, that he had then burned the house and that she had died in the byre five days thereafter. But Sellar was acquitted by a Scots jury of fifteen of whom the majority were landowners.

The result of the Sellar case showed nineteenth century Highland landlords and factors how far they could go.[1] It was a lesson which they were not slow to learn. The Disruption at least gave the Highlander the chance to reject the landowner's nominee as his minister. It is not surprising that he took it.

1. For information on this see Ian Grimble, *The Trial of Patrick Sellar.* (Routledge & Kegan Paul.)

13

Ecumenicity and Anglican Imperialism

I n writing about Anglican imperialism, one has to begin by making clear what in Anglicanism is being criticised and what is not. What is not being criticised is the quality of the Anglican Christian, both clerical and lay. If there are those who are unfortunate enough not to know Anglicans who are better Christians than they are, the present writer, one or two of whose closest friends belong to that communion, is not of their number. Nor is any attempt made here to deny that Anglicanism is one of the great indigenous churches of Christendom. Seldom indeed, can such a harmonious adjustment have been made between national behaviour patterns and a Christian way of life. As the name, Anglican, indicates, there is a quite unique bond between this particular country and this particular Christian denomination. Outside of England, Anglican churches have only taken root in countries which at some period have been occupied by an English army and governed by colonial adminstrators appointed by the English government. The non-Englishman listening to the conversation of clergy either of the Church of England or of a body such as the Episcopal Church of Scotland, becomes conscious of a curious world to which he does not belong. It is a world where it is a categorical imperative to send one's son to a boarding school and in which there are really only two universities. In the fantasy world of ecclesiastical power mythology, the Church of England bishops are the successors of the apostles. In the real world the most important thing about them is that—unlike Catholic bishops—they are almost exclusively public school products and graduates of Oxford and Cambridge. To all others the corridors of ecclesiastical power are strictly off limits.

For a church so strongly nationalistic to become imperialistically minded can obviously introduce disturbing and irrelevant considerations into the ecumenical debate. The tension between the nationalist and imperialist elements in Anglican policy is illustrated in a very moderate statement of it by a Scottish Episcopal bishop quoted in the *Scotsman* of 20th April 1961.

'Bishop E. F. Easson, speaking at the annual Synod of the Episcopal Church Diocese . . . in Aberdeen, on the efforts being made to achieve greater inter-Church unity, said yesterday that a great gulf still existed.

'On the one side was the Catholic section, represented by the Orthodox and Roman Catholic Churches, and on the other the Protestants represented by the type that would, in England, be classed as Nonconformist Churches.

'Between them we occupy a unique position', he said, 'for we are in a real sense both Catholic and Reformed. We find ourselves having to act as mediators between the two extremes. It is a position of the greatest delicacy and difficulty.'

The nationalistic element comes out in the way in which the bishop, though domiciled in Scotland and speaking there, and about to proceed to New Delhi, can only think of the interchurch situation in terms of an English setting. That setting is so untypical as to be highly misleading. One could, for instance, formulate a twentieth-century doctrine of church and state quite wrongly if one assumed that such notable resisters to totalitarianism as Bergrav, Barth and Bonhoeffer were Nonconformists. All three were ministers of a state church.

The imperialist element comes out in mild form in the way in which the Bishop assumes that his communion is to act as mediator in the debate between the Reformed and the Roman churches. Who asked it to be? The debate between Catholic and Reformed in Scotland is difficult and may well be long. But as long as the Anglicans keep out of it, it remains a debate about theological differences honestly held. It is only when the Anglicans intervene that the suspicion inevitably arises that one position put forward is not a theological one but simply that worship of English behaviour patterns which for so many years has been the basic idolatry of the Scottish upper middle classes.

Anglican imperialism is not of course exhausted by the claim to act as mediators between Catholic and Reformed. It occurs much more overtly, though even here under a facade of fine words in the ruthless series of take-over bids which the Church of England has been carrying out in the former English colonies and hopes soon to begin on the island itself. In ecumenical terminology these take-over bids are called church unions. But actually no term could be more inaccurate for the last thing the Anglicans want to do is to unite with Protestant ministers in the way e.g. that the ministers of the Church of Scotland wished to unite with those of the United Free Church in 1929. Anglicans do not wish to unite with Protestant ministers. They wish Protestant ministers to die off so that they can replace them with Anglican ones. Alternatively they wish to turn Protestant ministers into Anglican ones. These alternatives give rise to the two Anglican diplomatic techniques of the Dying-off period and Covert Ordination. In Ecumenical language these techniques are referred to as the South India method and the North India method.

The former technique is so macabre as to be fascinating. One can only regret that the conventions of ecumenical language have been allowed to conceal the role which death plays in the South India scheme. Clearly Anglican policy would be best served if Protestant ministers, after making their church over to the Anglicans, then at once carried out a simultaneous act of hara-kiri and allowed their successors to be ordained by Anglican bishops within the apostolic succession. But Anglicanism is a reasonable faith and this is not required of the uniting Protestants. Instead they are given a period of thirty years in which to die off. The fact that during this period a bishop consecrated by the Anglicans takes part in all ordinations secures their ultimate complete extinction. In the meantime apartheid and segregation hold sway. A kind of ecclesiastical Bantustan in the shape of the Church of South India is set up and with this at the present moment no province of the Church of England is in communion. But the parallel with South Africa must not be pressed unduly. In this case the segregation is only temporary and will be terminated with the death of the last Protestant minister. At the deathbed of this aged divine the Anglicans will be waiting with the vultures. His last breath will be the signal for rejoicing to break out that no longer do any barriers stand in the way of the complete union of the Church of South India and the Anglican Communion. At the wedding breakfast of the queen bee, the bridegroom, for the best of reasons, is conspicuous by his absence. The same phenomenon will characterise the final celebrations over the union of South India, even if, in this case, the wedding breakfast is postponed thirty years.

Many sensitive Anglicans will be repelled at this description of Anglican diplomatic action. This is all to the good if their revulsion is felt for the action and not for the description. The action is of course ascribed by the Anglican diplomats and their ecumenical fellow-travellers to the Will of God. But this, as we have seen in earlier chapters, is simply the age-old ecclesiastical device for drawing attention away from less reputable agencies at work in the church. In this case, the agency made use of is simply that of the Grim Reaper. The embrace of the Anglicans is indeed the kiss of death. But any Hollywood undertaker would envy them the skill with which they conceal the fact that their Loved Ones are, if not the mortui, at least the morituri.

Basically then, Anglican diplomatic policy is the extermination of all Protestant (i.e. non-episcopally ordained) ministers. On the South India scheme this is secured by the strangling of all Protestant ministers at birth by the simple expedient of securing the presence and operation of an Anglican consecrated bishop at their ordination. All present Protestant ministers are left to the Grim Reaper to deal with in his own slow but nevertheless sure way. But there is an alternative to this buying deaths with time scheme. It is the North India plan, for which the Covert Ordination technique is earmarked. Where this is employed, the ministers of the non-Anglican church (it may so desire, protesting up to the last their previous ordination) are ordained by Anglican bishops at an inauguration service, which must be described as a masterpiece of double-think. The Protestant ministers may protest quite sincerely that they have already been ordained. But this does not worry the Anglicans who know that they have not been and are now going to be. The confusion of such a preposterous inauguration service is increased by the fact that some Anglicans can say with sincerity that they receive as well as give at such a service. But whatever they conceive of themselves of receiving it is not the gift of essential ministry. They see the inauguration service as like the meeting of two ships' lifeboats on the morning after the ship has gone down. The one lifeboat contains two kegs of water, the other two gramophones, and at their meeting a keg of water is exchanged for a gramophone.

So much for the alternative north-India scheme of covert ordination. That its inauguration service can only be described as a fiesta of double-think points to a basic flaw in the ecumenical movement—the divorce between ecumenical actions and ecumenical language. Ecumenical language is framed not to describe but to conceal ecumenical actions. This is inevitable. For the Anglican diplomats take the view (which is not necessarily that of all Anglicans) that their ministers are real ministers and Protestant ministers are not. Progress can therefore only be made by the extinction of all Protestant ministers, and all Anglican schemes are schemes for just that. But they obviously cannot be so described by Anglicans and their fellow travellers, otherwise they would not take place. Hence ecumenical language and ecumenical actions must diverge and anyone who at a truly ecumenical gathering tries to correlate the two is soon made aware that he has said the wrong thing.

If one basic need of the Anglican diplomats and their fellow-travellers is a language which conceals the nature of ecumenical events, another is a timetable. It seems evident that Anglican diplomacy has lined the Protestant churches up for extinction in a very definite order. First come those in the former English colonies followed by those in England itself. These are relatively easy meat in view of the comparative numerical strength of the Anglicans in these countries and the further advantage which Anglicans enjoy because of the way in which social values

determine English thinking. In assessing the power relation between the Church of X and the Church of Y, it is important to
ask whether the establishment of the Church of X looks up to the
establishment of the Church of Y socially or vice versa. In
England there is not much doubt as to how this relation stands
between Church of England top brass and non-conformist top
brass. This is a tremendous asset to the Church of England and
its present ambitious diplomatic phase.

The case is very different when we come to the United States
and the Continent of Europe. In the United States the Anglicans
are in a marked minority and on the Continent of Europe they
simply do not exist. Nor is there either in the United States or
on the Continent axiomatic acceptance of the standards of the
English class system. It is therefore clear that in the Anglican
power drive Scotland and Canada have an important position.
They represent the soft underbelly of Protestantism. It is true
that in both these countries, and particularly in Scotland,
Anglicans are very much in a minority. But there is sufficient
deference to the imperatives of the English class structure to
make victory a reasonable possibility.

This can only be doubted by those who do not face up to the
part which power plays in ecclesiastical diplomacy. The
Anglicans have something to offer their fellow-travellers and
that something is power. 'Gaiters for the boys' is not a bad
description of how the Ecumenical Movement appears to the
ambitious Protestant ecclesiastic. And before the Ecumenical
puts this page down in horror let him ask whether the call for
sacrifice so often reiterated in the esoteric language of his movement had ever been matched in the realm of action by the
surrender by a single ecclesiastic of a single particle of power.
We have, I understand, in the Ecumenical Movement, a
Presbyterian minister who has become a bishop. There is, of
course, nothing remarkable in that. What would be remarkable
would be a Pope who became Bishop of Barchester or a Bishop
of Barchester who became minister of Auchentogle. And of that
there is no sign whatever.

To stress the part which power plays in ecclesiastical policies
is not to yield to unchristian cynicism but simply to face one of

the facts of life. Anyone training men for the Protestant ministry to-day must make it clear to them that in embarking on this career they are sacrificing all prospects of having power. The trouble is that the desire for power is one of the temptations, not of youth, but of middle age. It is only in that phase of life that the Protestant minister, visiting perhaps the executive office of some once less talented former schoolfellow with its light screen of subordinates summoned by a word on a secretary's telephone, realises the extent of the sacrifice he has made on ordination. It would be unreasonable to expect all competent middle aged Protestant ministers to have the wisdom to see that the influence which a good minister possesses is something much more precious than power. And if that is so, it would be folly to deny that an ecclesiastical establishment which has bishoprics to offer has more bargaining power than one which has not. Nor is it the case the episcopal gaiters have an appeal only to those Protestant ministers for whom an Anglican take-over bid affords reasonable prospects of wearing them. Their attraction for the less competent Protestant minister is different but equally real. The prospect of being able to call in someone who can bring to heel a Kirk Session or Diaconate with whom he is estranged can present itself as an easy way out of his difficulties.

Anglican imperialism has thus techniques, a timetable and bargaining powers. Frankly, it needs all three. For the audacity of this venture in ecclesiastical imperialism is all the more striking when it is stripped of the cover of ecumenical language which conceals it. Like their Elizabethan ancestors the English empire-builders of to-day work from a relatively weak base. The Church of England membership compared to the size of population of the country is not large and compares unfavourably with the comparable figures for the Church of Scotland. But by grading the series of take-over bids so as to proceed from the easier to the more difficult (thus Methodism has to be taken over before the Church of Scotland), the final goal will ultimately be achieved, when with the extinction and absorption of all the Protestant Churches the Church of England will be able to meet the power of the Roman Catholic Church on something like equal terms.

It only remains to say something about the motives for this sustained and ambitious chapter in ecclesiastical imperialism. The motives which the Anglicans and their fellow-travellers ascribe to themselves in Ecumenical literature are of the highest, being devotion to the Will of God or the Holy Spirit. Up till now this intriguing lack of modesty has paid off. It is only recently that the public has begun to react to the Ecumenical's unending professions of enthusiasm for the Will of God and the Holy Spirit with faint but unmistakable signs of nausea.

Certainly if the argument of this book has shown anything, it has led us to query the identification of devotion to the Will of God and the motive for the series of accomplished and projected Anglican take-over bids which up till now has been the practical outcome of the Ecumenical Movement. For one thing, we have seen how long before the rise of the Ecumenical Movement the Will of God has been the time-honoured device whereby the ecclesiastical operator at once intensified and concealed his imperialistic drives and canonized his unchristian hatreds. In the language of personal religion the Will of God is a term which deserves the highest respect. Which of us would not take seriously the statement of a friend who told us that he had come to accept that some accident or illness was God's will for him? But in ecclesiastical politics the Will of God is a device to enable sinful man to evade the imperative of love. And further it has been the contention of this book that ecumenical language differs from ordinary language in that its aim is not to describe but to conceal actions. Of no two expressions is this more true than the Will of God and the Holy Spirit. The reader would be remarkably naïve if he took them at their face value as they appear in ecumenical documents. This may seem a harsh statement if we think of the new and commendable spirit of friendship between people of different denominations. But we are not concerned here with this spirit of friendship but with the ecclesiastical mergers which profess to express but often exploit it. The friendship of individual Christians of different denominations is one thing, ecclesiastical diplomacy is another and very different one.

The motives for the present mood of Anglican imperialism

are rather to be found in much more prosaic and human considerations. One of them is the conviction which many Anglicans have that theirs is the Church halfway between Catholicism and Protestantism. This genuine conviction, sincerely held, almost unconsciously commits those who hold it to an imperialist policy. For it leads logically to the view that Church union is to be effected by Catholics and Protestants becoming Anglicans and Anglicans remaining as they are.

The Church of England, however, is less a midway Church than a nationalistic one and it reflects fairly faithfully the characteristics of the English people. One of the less attractive of these has been unkindly described as arrogance. It is seen in the quaint devices in which the universities of Oxford and Cambridge recognise each other in a way in which they recognise no other university. But if this is arrogance, it is arrogance which in the age of the University of California and Academic City, Siberia, had grown rather pitiful. It is therefore perhaps more charitable to refer to this basic attitude of the English as institutional narcissism. The doctrine of apostolic succession enables Englishmen to give expression to institutional narcissism in the ecclesiastical orb just as the romanticisation of Oxford and Cambridge has enabled them to do so in the academic one. The doctrine of apostolic succession does not, it is true, enable Anglicans to assert the superiority of their own ecclesiastical behaviour patterns to those of France and Spain. But then these countries have not, subsequent to the Tractarian Movement, been serious rivals to England, as the more Protestant powers of Germany and America have been. One of the main functions of the doctrine of Apostolic Succession in England to-day is that it enables Anglicans to find expression in their references to German Protestantism for national anti-German sentiment.[1] Thus English institutional narcissism provides a main key to the activities carried on by Anglican diplomacy under the cloak of Ecumenicity. Nor can one neglect the part Apostolic Succession plays in enabling Englishmen to live with the post-1945 Anglo-American power relationship. In an age when the Englishman suddenly found himself no longer

1. For reference of Anglican writers to German theology see pp. 159-161.

able to patronise the American as a Colonial, it is natural and understandable that there should be a good deal of the Nietzschean resentment of the weak for the strong in the English attitude to the United States. It was this resentment, for instance, which became too much for Maclean and Burgess to bear and it can be observed in countless less dramatic instances. The doctrine of Apostolic Succession gives at least partial relief to this resentment by enabling the Englishman to look down on the Protestantism of the American power groups. In an era when the military institutions of Messrs. Eisenhower and Dulles were only too painfully superior, it could not fail to be a small compensation to dwell on the inferiority of their religious ones. This exercise to which English Ecumenicals were not unaddicted was not altogether easy in view of the obvious fact that American Churches were much better attended than English ones. To be able to set this aside as quite irrelevant and still to assert the superiority of English Church life over American is an important function which the doctrine of Apostolic Succession can fulfil for the Anglican.

Whatever the motives of Anglican imperialism there is no doubt as to its nature. There are two million communicants in the Church of England.[1] In Scotland there are 56,000[1] Anglicans and in the United States 2,174,202 (one in every 86 of the population).[1] On the Continent of Europe the number of Anglicans is as near nil as to make no odds. In all these countries the Protestant Churches are to submit to a complete reconstruction of their power structure and the extinction of their present ministry and its replacement by Anglican ordained clergy in order to conform to the preferences of 2 million Englishmen. This is one of the most grotesque manifestations of twentieth century racialism. That such a project should be taking the Christians mind off the vital tasks of evangelisation and apologetics is a scandalous waste of time. That it should be dignified with the name of the purpose of God is irreverent in the extreme.

1. These figures are taken respectively from the 'Anatomy of Britain', from Dr. John Highet's 'The Churches in Scotland' and from a letter from Professor John Macquarrie to the *Church Times*.

14

Coronation Canossa

Painful though the account must be, the story of the General Assembly Moderator's part in the Coronation of 1953 has to be told. There can be little doubt that this melancholy incident must have done much to convince Fisher and the other English bishops that there was no limit to the ignominy which could be inflicted on the Church of Scotland now that its diplomacy was under the control of the pro-Anglican or Ecumenical party.

At the time most of the details of the incident were kept secret by the Anglicans and their Ecumenical fellow-travellers in the Church of Scotland. But thirteen years later an account of the matter in a small book of essays, *Evangelicals and Unity* and quoted in the Scottish Daily Express moved Fisher, the English Archbishop, to defend his part in the affair in a letter to that paper. (17.2.60). Here is what he writes about his arrangement of this Coronation Service.

'So far as Doctrine was concerned, I detached the giving of the Bible from a doctrinally wrong place and put it where, as I thought, it properly belonged. Then having ascertained that there was no legal objection to my doing so, with the Queen's approval, I invited my dear friend, Dr. Pitt-Watson, then Moderator, to present the Bible.'

Translated out of ecumenical jargon this probably means that before he asked The Moderator of the General Assembly to take a very small part in the Coronation, he took good care to see that part was moved out of the Communion Service.

So much for the invitation. It arrived in Edinburgh at a time

when Anglo-Scottish relations were not at their best. The
nationalisms of both countries had recently been fanned by
diverse factors. England in that Coronation year of 1953 was
still hardly conscious that she had ceased to be a great power
but was increasingly impatient of the continuing wartime
restrictions and rationing, a thing of the past to Germany,
her defeated enemy. To the English the accession of the young
monarch seemed to bring promise of a new Elizabethan age
with England again taking the lead in exploration and a power
among the nations. Not having prophetic vision they were able
to bask in the first conquest of Everest and were spared the fore-
knowledge of Russian and American sputnik travel and such
events as the annexation of Rockall, the Iceland cod-war and
the battle of Port Said. For the Scots, on the other hand, the
years when their meat ration had been inferior both in quantity
and quality had been the years when the ever increasing prices
paid by foreign buyers at Perth bull sales testified that their
beef was the best in the world. Difficulties in foreign exchange
were put forward as reasons why for instance there was a long
waiting list for motor cars. But nobody doubted that whisky
and tweed were excellent dollar earners. The suspicion had
grown that Scotland might be economically better without her
southern neighbour.

Out of this mood had grown the success of John McCormick's
covenant with its demand for Scottish Self-Government.
Occasionally the mood seemed as if it might erupt into action.
There was some talk of a Scottish Republican Army. In 1953
certain shopkeepers who in their coronation decorations in-
serted the numeral II after the monarch's name were liable to
have a stone thrown through their window and pillar boxes
with the like offending numeral were on occasion treated with
explosives.

None of these events led to actual bodily injury but there is no
doubt that they made the authorities jumpy. The Coronation
Year was not to go past without trial and conviction of Edinburgh students for alleged action against the Crown. One of the
crown witnesses was alleged to be a police informer and it
would be interesting after this passage of time to see the whole

case examined by a competent journalist or legal historian. Certainly when two years earlier the King had been due to visit the University of Glasgow on the occasion of its fifth centenary, the elaborate security precautions could only be described as preposterous. The King's illness unfortunately prevented his attendance. The absence of a member of the Royal Family at the fifth centenary of Britain's fourth oldest university was commented on by many among the large body of very distinguished academic figures from all over the world who did make the journey to Glasgow. No doubt quite erroneously it was connected by some of them with the removal by Glasgow students of the Stone of Destiny from Westminster Abbey which had taken place a few years previously.

The original stealing of this venerable relic from Scone Abbey had been one of the rather less revolting war crimes of the Plantagenet English King Edward I, in comparison with his murdering of P.O.W.'s, his torturing of women prisoners by hanging them from cages and his barbarous execution of the Scottish patriot, Wallace. The stealing of a stone, whatever its associations, is perhaps hardly worth bothering about. Even so, one would have thought that the proximity of the loot of so nauseating a war criminal to the high altar in a consecrated building would have been a source of embarrassment. It is hard for instance to imagine the Archbishop of Cologne allowing his cathedral to be adorned by the paintings stolen by the Nazis from the countries they invaded. The reaction of the Dean of Westminster was very different though, lest even for a moment we seem to suggest that an Englishman can be spiritually less sensitive than a German, it must be stressed that he was a Scotsman in whose upbringing all the factors making for deracination had played their part. A product of the Scottish Episcopal Church, a product of an English school and university, his antipathy to any expression of the nationalism of his country, however harmless, provided the only explanation of his conduct. Going to the microphone of the B.B.C. he made an impassioned appeal for the return of this dubious piece of church furnishing to his place of worship.

As sometimes happens, the action of the civil authorities was more restrained than that of the ecclesiastical. Once the Stone of Destiny had been returned to the police, the London Government took no action against the young nationalists who had removed it. Further, the rumour went around, that if the Church of Scotland wished the stone to be returned to Scotland apart from its use at coronations, this could be arranged. If such a hint was indeed given by the London Government, the Church of Scotland's reaction to it provides an outstanding instance of its anti-nationalist syndrome. When the Convener of the Church and Nations Committee, the distinguished ecclesiastical historian, Professor J. H. S. Burleigh, proposed that the Stone of Destiny be returned to Scotland, his proposal aroused in the Assembly an ugly scene which will long remain in the memory of those who witnessed it. Not only was the proposal overwhelmingly defeated but the demand was made that all reference to the matter be deleted from the Church and Nation Committee's Report. This was a virtually unheard of snub to the Committee and its Convenor and Professor Burleigh would have been justified in handing in his resignation on the spot. The whole incident is a curious sidelight on the pathology of Scotland. Had the Stone of Destiny been taken by the English from Ghana or Malawi, the General Assembly would have been insistent that it be returned thither. The powerful pro-African Foreign Mission Committee which was to do so much to destroy Rhodesian Federation in the interests of Malawi nationalism, would have seen to that. But the young nationalists who took the Stone of Destiny from Westminster had committed the solecism not only of not having black faces but actually of being Scottish. In the circumstances it was inevitable that the Assembly should repudiate their action with the utmost vehemence.

The outcome of this debate must have gone far to justify Dr. Pitt-Watson's acceptance of the Archbishop's invitation to take part in the Coronation Service at Westminster Abbey. Had the Dean of Westminster reacted against an African nationalist gesture, the Foreign Mission Committee might well have had misgivings about the Moderator taking part in so public a service with him. But in the circumstances all was well and one can hardly charge Dr. Pitt-Watson with going counter to the wishes of his Church. That these coincided with his own, there can be little doubt. As one of the ablest leaders of the Ecumenical Party, he was to sign the Bishops' Report and finally to bemoan its defeat over the B.B.C. network. But whether even a leader of the Ecumenical Party could be entirely happy about the indignities heaped on him by the Anglicans at the Coronation is doubtful. It is significant that Professor Pitt-Watson never told the full story of what transpired during his lifetime and the present writer, though a colleague of his, never learned it until Archbishop Fisher was provoked by the Scottish Daily Express into relating and defending his actions. If the other leaders of the Ecumenical party knew the full story of what happened to their Moderator at the Coronation, they were careful not to divulge it.

The part allotted to the Moderator at the Coronation was pathetic in its brevity. He had to say a few words and hand a Bible to the Queen. Much more serious was the fact that during its performance he, as the representative of the Church of Scotland knelt in a place of worship, but did not kneel to God. Further, having been manoeuvred by the Anglicans into a position that they would never have got a Catholic Cardinal to assume, the unfortunate Pitt-Watson was photographed in it.

Now there is no doubt that Dr. Pitt-Watson was a romantic and passionate royalist and as a private individual he was entitled to express his devotion to the Monarch in any way he pleased. But having accepted the Chair of the Supreme Court of the national Church he was under an obligation to observe its traditions. And kneeling before monarchs is not one of them. The only parallel to the incident was the melancholy one where another distinguished Scotsman, the Earl of Moray, was made by the first Elizabeth to grovel before her in the presence of the French and Spanish Ambassadors. It may well be that Pitt-Watson was ignorant of this incident and perhaps also of the biting words in which one of his predecessors, George Buchanan, in his great defence of democracy, the *De Jure Regni apud Scotos*, had compared a king at his Coronation to a girl's doll. But he knew well enough that Knox's Nathan-like refusal to recognise the monarch as head of the Church lived on in the General Assembly's careful arrangement that it is neither opened nor closed by the monarch's representative. In the circumstances Pitt-Watson's acceptance of this particular part in the Coronation is inexplicable. It is not necessarily that the traditions of his Church were beyond criticism. But the Coronation was not the moment, nor had Pitt-Watson the authority to flout them as flagrantly as he did.

Besides being compelled by his posture to acknowledge the Monarch as Head of the Church, a doctrine asserted by the Anglican Church and denied by his own, further humiliation was heaped on the Moderator at the Coronation. Not only had steps apparently been taken to see that his insignificant share of the Coronation was removed from the Communion Service but at that service the elements of bread and wine were deliberately withheld from him by Fisher, the English Archbishop. In his belated account of the matter the latter does not say whether the unfortunate Pitt-Watson was given any warning of this fresh humiliation meted out to him. Certainly the experience of being without warning refused the communion elements by the officiating priest or minister is an experience so infrequent and shattering as to be traumatic. Such a deep and serious wound inflicted on him and not simply the interests of Ecumenical party policy may well explain Pitt-Watson's reluctance to mention the incident. And indeed Ecumenical party leader though he was he may have retained sufficient loyalty to see the incident as a slight to the Church which he represented, at whose every Communion Service an invitation goes out to believers of all denominations.

It is certainly no part of the present work to account for the net of silence so long kept over the incident by the motive least creditable to James Pitt-Watson who besides being a zealous ecclesiastical politician was something of a romantic idealist.

Now that the silence has at long last been broken, we cannot acquit him of failing to maintain the traditions and theological position of the Church of Scotland at that great fiesta of tradition and Anglican theology, the Coronation. For this his membership of the Ecumenical party was to blame. For the rest one can only regret the humiliations which his Anglican friends whose interests he was later to serve to the hurt of his own Church chose to heap on him on this occasion. And one must regret that the occasion which they chose to inflict this Canossa in reverse on a Scots Moderator was one so important to their nation and their Royal Family.

NOTE ABOUT DR. PITT-WATSON: I have been asked to add the information that the decision to take part in the Coronation Ceremony was made not by Dr. Pitt-Watson but by the General Administration Committee of the Church of Scotland. I do this gladly in the interests of accuracy and in fairness to the memory of an esteemed colleague.

I. H.

15

The Bishops' Report

THE first serious attempt of Anglican imperialism to take over the Church of Scotland came to a head in 1957 with the publication of a Joint Report. This report, later to be called in Scotland, the Bishops' Report, was signed by twelve representatives of the Church of England, twelve of the Church of Scotland, three of the Episcopal Church in Scotland and four of the Presbyterian Church of England. The Report, as one of the Scottish signatories accurately predicted a few months before its publication, came as a bombshell in the Church of Scotland. The reason for this was that that Church had not realised what a stranglehold the Ecumenical party had gained over its diplomacy. Nor had it realised just how far that party was prepared to go in signing a Report which can only be called an ecclesiastical Munich.

On the other side of the Border the document was admirably calculated not to cause the slightest ripple at a vicarage tea party. The only approach to a concession which the Anglicans made in the report, a vague promise to introduce something like the eldership into their system, they subsequently never even bothered to discuss among themselves. It is hard to believe that they ever had the slightest intention to implement it.

There was nothing vague about the concession the Kirk was to have to make. Bishops, duly consecrated into the apostolic succession, were to be set up as permanent moderators of presbyteries. This was quite a drastic alteration of the power structure of the Church of Scotland. The moderator of a presbytery was to be changed from being a mere temporary chairman into someone whom it would be injudicious to disagree with, if one valued one's professional future. This is a matter where it is foolish to shut one's eyes to the naked reality of power. A chairman who can affect the professional futures of his committee members, adversely or otherwise, is much more likely to get his way with them that one who cannot.

If the Church of Scotland representatives apparently did not notice this formidable transformation and concentration of power proposed for their own church, it must be said in extenuation that it did not affect the majority of them personally. Six of the eleven ministerial representatives of the Kirk were not in the parish ministry but in the university service. No presbytery moderator permanent or otherwise was going to interfere with their professional future. It is amusing that the one place where the Anglicans found their Church of Scotland fellow-negotiators insufficiently amenable was on the one point where the new power concentration might affect the life of academic teachers of theology. In the separate contribution which they make to the report, the Anglican representatives write: '. . . there might be anxiety if the place of Bishops as collectively having a necessary voice in matters of doctrine were not safeguarded.' There might well be. Anyone fortunate enough to know the late Professor John Baillie will find it hard to envisage him allowing any Presbytery Moderator to lay down what was to be taught in the Divinity department of the University of Edinburgh.

If we pass from naked power to institutions the one-sided nature of the Bishops' Report is equally evident. The Union of 1707 had left only two Scottish institutions intact, the Church and the Law. The presbyterian constitution of the former had been expressly written into the legislation of the Treaty of Union. Now, exactly 250 years after the Union, eleven ministers and one lawyer were prepared to sell that pitiful remnant of the birthright, apparently ignorant even after that winter of Suez, that the supply of pottage in London was running out. The controversy which the Bishops' Report provoked in Scotland was the kind which would arise in England if the Archbishop of

Canterbury were to propose that adult baptism be introduced into the Church of England to facilitate union with the great Southern Baptist Communion in the U.S. or if the Head of Eton were to propose that his and similar schools were to be modified in certain important respects to bring them into line with American co-educational high schools.

It is perhaps one of the secrets of England's greatness that her responsible leaders do not make this kind of proposal to alter their country's institutions in order to conform with those of a neighbour, however friendly or powerful. Behind this attitude is Burke's insight that institutions are organic growths changing in the light of their own laws but not so susceptible to alteration on principles laid down from without. Burke chided the French revolutionaries for having overthrown the institutions of their own country. He told them that he had no desire to see these native French institutions replaced by copies of English ones. And it is significant that so fine an interpreter of England as Sir Arthur Bryant did not seem to come down on the side of the bishops-in-presbytery proposal in the course of two sensitive articles he wrote after a visit to the General Assembly during the period. But there was nothing of the wisdom of Burke and Bryant's organic philosophy of institutions in Anglican ecclesiastical imperialism bent to extinguish one of Scotland's few remaining institutions.

But there is a world of difference between the wise and measured English patriotism of Burke and Bryant and the coarse Anglican imperialism of the ecumenical era. No less a person than the editor of Crockford accused the Church of Scotland of nationalism for rejecting the Bishops' Report, and refusing to allow itself to be reconstituted on lines approved of in Canterbury. To anyone who has read the earlier chapters of this book nationalism will seem an incredible label to fix on the Church of Scotland. Cradled in treason, impelled by its Old Testament blueprint to turn Scotland from a nation into a church, a body which could have prevented the Union of 1707 but did not, the Church of Scotland has only rarely in a Chalmers approached the English patriotism which finds its finest expression in a Burke and a Bryant but which in some form enlivens every English institution from the English church to the English pub. But in fairness to the Editor of Crockford it must be pointed out that every imperialist finds those of another nation who oppose his designs to be animated by a most perverse nationalism. No doubt Jezebel thought of Elijah as a most pernicious nationalist. And when one considers the strength and vigour with which the great English institutions have survived two great wars, the attempt which English churchmen made in the Bishops' Report to destroy one of few remaining ones of a smaller and neighbour country can only be described as a kind of operation Naboth's Vineyard.

Needless to say, this is not how the Bishops' Report appeared to the Church of Scotland delegates who signed this. They were able and intelligent men who produced a document which is a classic of diplomatic ineptitude. In part this paradox is to be explained in terms of their class. The viewpoint which they represented was for the most part that of the Edinburgh professors and the fashionable Edinburgh churches. It was hardly representative of the Church of Scotland as a whole. It was that of upper middle class Scotland rather than middle middle class Scotland. And the basic principle of the religion of upper middle class Scotland is that English institutions are U and Scottish institutions are non-U. From that basic principle, a document like the Bishops' Report follows with inexorable logic. At an early period in the present writer's academic career, he was startled when at the conclusion of a not-unimpressive University function, a leading Scottish churchman turned to him and said 'Wouldn't this all be so much better if it were done in England'. Seven years later the speaker was to be one of the ablest and most likable signatories and champions of the Bishops' Report.

Even though their diplomatic activity was a catastrophe whose extent cannot yet be measured, it is impossible not to feel some sympathy for the signatories of the Bishops' Report. Themselves but the latest manifestation of the curious anti-nationalist syndrome which has run through Scottish history, they could hardly be expected to see that the anti-nationalism of the past had made Scots people feel very passionately about their church. After all, if you turn the nation into a church, are you not going to turn the church into a nation? It was one of the few institutions left to the Scots to feel passionately about. Again the Scottish Bishops' Report signatories while in some cases possessing considerable theological ability seem to have been completely ignorant of sociological factors. They transferred the whole discussion from the field of culture to that of faith. [1] In this they were quite disastrously abetted by the Church of Scotland Inter-Church Relations Committee, a different body from that which with its Anglican co-delegates had produced the Bishops' Report, but, at the time, also under the convenership of Dr. A. C. Craig. One unintentionally but appallingly exacerbating factor in the controversy was the statement which the Inter-Church Relations Committee prefaced to its comments on the Bishops' Report in 1958. It ran as follows:

'The Committee desired to preface its comments on the Joint Report by recording its unanimous conviction that the full and visible unity of all Christian people is a primary implication of the Gospel: that, when fully realised, such unity will mean one Church in place of the many existing denominations: that prayer for the overcoming of existing disunity is a primary obligation of Christian discipleship: and that such prayer must remain unreal unless it issue in earnest and unremitting efforts to break down all barriers to unity, however caused.

Equally we are convinced that only a united Christendom can bear full witness to the One Lord of the Church and serve Him as He wills to be served, and that our existing divisions seriously hamper and weaken the work of evangelism. Hence, the efforts toward unity being made in our day, of which the Joint Report is a striking product, must be regarded, not as a secondary concern and responsibility of the Church, but as a duty bound up with that of evangelism, and, equally with it, laid by Christ upon His people.'

1. The difference between a concern of faith and a concern of culture has been made very clearly by my colleague, Dr. Allan Galloway, in his yet unpublished Kerr Lectures of 1966.

Now the opposite of these propositions can at least be argued, both empirically and exegetically. Church attendance figures are considerably higher in the United States, where there are more denominations than in Sweden, where there is virtually only one. Perhaps divisions aren't such a hindrance to the evangelism of modern man. And it may be that when our Lord expressed His will that we be all one, His demand was that we should all love one another. But leaving arguments aside, by stating that the will of Christ is that there be one church, the Inter-Church Relations Committee inevitably, though I am sure unintentionally, tended to imply that to oppose some such measures as those put forward by the Joint Report was to oppose Christ. Those who supported the proposals were thus exposed to the temptation of treating those who differed from them as men who were opposing Christ. That temptation was often nobly withstood. But the temptation inherent in the above statement to treat those who opposed the Craig report as enemies of God was not always resisted by the Ecumenicals.

The result was that during the years 1957 to 1959 the Ecumenicals plunged Scotland into a controversy so acrimonious as to give satisfaction only to those opposed to Christianity.

Here, for instance, is an account of a meeting of the Presbytery of Kilmarnock in January, 1958:

'A Scots professor attacked Lord Beaverbrook and the *Scottish Daily Express* last night over the Bishops-in-the-Kirk report.

He is the Rev. Professor T. F. Torrance, of New College, Edinburgh—one of the authors of the report—and he indicated to Kilmarnock Presbytery that it looked as though the plan was already defeated at Presbytery level. But he went on: "In spite of all the pressures and the fanatics—and we have a lunatic fringe—the General Assembly as a rule is remarkably free and open to the guidance of God. I would only hope that that will happen."

Professor Torrance complained: "The Christian is at a distinct disadvantage against Satan. The difficulty is that at the beginning of any battle like this, Satan tries to jockey for the dominant position and win it before the battle is enjoined and it looks like that now." [1]

At first sight one is almost grateful for this utterance. For the thought of the mild Dr. George Dryburgh, the main critic of the Bishops' Report, taking his instructions from a horned figure in red tights, is so absurd as to be deliriously funny. But second thoughts are vastly sadder. Professor Torrance is not all comic relief. The man who ascribed opposition to a manifesto drawn up by himself and some twenty others as Satan jockeying for position, is going a long way toward creating a certain type of atmosphere. It is the atmosphere where it is scarcely possible for reasonable men to discuss or Christians to speak the truth in love.

For two years the Bishops' Report controversy dragged on, distracting the attention of the Church of Scotland from the vastly more important tasks of evangelising and adapting its approach to meet the situation created by the post-war industrial society. The proposals in the report introduced into Scottish ecclesiastical life an acrimony which had been absent from it for fifty years. By identifying their party policy with the will of God, the Ecumenical party had found the formula, which, as earlier chapters have shown, has unfailingly proved disastrous for the Church of Scotland. It was such an identification of their policy with the Crown Rights of the Redeemer by the Evangelical Party which broke the Church of Scotland in two in 1843. Inevitably the Bishops' Report controversy left behind it the small gnawing fear that the good work of 1929 might be undone and conceivably the Church of Scotland might break again.

In the end the Bishops' Report proposals were rejected by the

1. This quotation is from the *Scottish Daily Express* of 28th January 1958. The question of the reliability of this paper's reporting of Ecumenical happenings is discussed in detail in Chapters 16 and 17. Here we need only note that the above report tallies with that given of the same Presbytery meeting on 1st February 1958 by the Kilmarnock Standard, a journal which has hitherto escaped censure in the Convocation of Canterbury. The Kilmarnock Standard account adds that Mr McAra (a member of Presbytery) objected to the word 'critic' being coupled with the word 'devil'.

General Assembly. There was some talk among Ecumenicals as to whether the decision involved a departure by the Church of Scotland from the Lausanne Declaration according to which bishops are to be a feature of the Church of the future. The discussion revealed a curious ignorance of the Church of Scotland constitution on which one might have expected the Ecumenical party chiefs to be able to illuminate their Anglican friends. One basic feature of the constitution of the Church of Scotland is the Barrier Act which goes back to 1697. This act lays down that all changes in doctrine and constitution must secure not only a majority in the General Assembly but also be approved by a majority of the Presbyteries in the Church. The Lausanne Declaration which clearly envisages a church of a different constitution from that of the present Church of Scotland has never gone to Presbyteries for approval. It has therefore never been accepted by the Church of Scotland.

The defeat of the Bishops' Report in the General Assembly was interpreted by Dr. A. C. Craig as the rejection of his policy. He therefore immediately tendered his resignation from the Convenership of the Inter-Church Relations Committee. That he promptly took this very honourable step was a personally most creditable gesture on the part of Dr. Craig. It was rendered politically nugatory by the immediate appointment as his successor of another Ecumenical member and signatory of the Bishops' Report. The Ecumenical party chiefs were resolved that the Assembly's decision was not going to interfere too much with their schemes for serving the interests of their Anglican friends. It is true that they were faced with the difficulty that the Assembly laid down that the next round of talks with Anglicans was to be confined to four abstract subjects and not to involve any concrete schemes for union with the Anglican Church. How the Ecumenical party tried to get round that one forms the fascinating story of the Holland House Plan. It will be dealt with in Chapter 16.

But before we leave the Bishops' Report, let us note a postscript which underlines its ineptitude as an Anglo-Scottish ecclesiastical settlement. It is contained in a sentence in the Lambeth Report which runs:

'It must, however, be recognised as a fact that Anglicans conscientiously hold that the celebrant of the Eucharist should have been ordained by a bishop standing in the historic succession, and generally believe it to be their duty to bear witness to this principle by receiving Holy Communion only from those who have been thus ordained.'

One great merit of this statement is that it contains the recognition, somewhat rare in Ecumenical documents, that Christians have consciences and that it may be this fact and not sin, which keeps them from being in the same denomination.

But from our immediate standpoint the important thing about the sentence quoted from the Lambeth Report is that it shows that even if the Church of Scotland had accepted the Bishops' Report it would not be in inter-communion with any Anglican church. It would have been like the Church of South India, an ecclesiastical Bantustan, condemned to thirty years of Apartheid. From the Anglican standpoint it was not enough for the present ministers of the Church of Scotland to accept the Bishops' Report. They had to do one thing more—they had to die—all of them, not just the caddish unhelpful ones like the present writer, but the good helpful ones like Dr. Craig. Until that happy event takes place, Anglicans, the Lambeth Report assures us, cannot with a clear conscience take communion in the Church of Scotland, bishops in presbytery or no bishops in presbytery.

Well, if that is the Anglican conscience one must respect it. But is it too much to ask Anglicans in return to remember that consciences grow on both sides of the Border? And there are certainly those in the Church of Scotland who cannot conscientiously agree with the Lambeth principle which would have kept the average Englishman from receiving Holy Communion at the hands of not a few of the greatest Christian ministers of this century, to some of whom God has given the crown of martyrdom.

16

The Holland House Affair

THE official Report of the Dougall-Tomkins conversations says 'we see God's mercy in the way in which His Spirit is leading us to seek new patterns of Church life'. It would be a pity if the reader were denied a closer view of the operation of the Holy Spirit through a curious reticence on the part of the Report about a certain phase of the conversations.

Holland House is a residence of the University of Edinburgh. From the 5th to the 7th of January 1966 it was to be the scene of a conference which marked the culmination of conversations between a Church of England Committee (whose convener was Dr. Tomkins, Bishop of Bristol), a committee of the same size of the Church of Scotland (its convener was Dr. Dougall) and smaller committees of the Episcopal Church in Scotland and the Presbyterian Church of England.

The Church of Scotland committee which was to take part in the Holland House Conference is officially known as the Special Committee. It was appointed by the General Assembly after Dr. Craig's Bishops' Report (officially called the Joint Report) had been rejected by that body, and it had a much more limited function than Dr. Craig's committee. It was appointed not to bring forward any plans for union between the Church of Scotland and an Episcopal Church, but simply to discuss four subjects with the Anglicans. The General Assembly of 1959 laid down that before further progress can be made 'certain issues require to be clarified and resolved . . . the chief among which concern (a) the meaning of unity as distinct from uniformity in Church order; (b) the meaning of "validity" as applied to ministerial orders; (c) the doctrine of Holy Communion and (d) the meaning of the Apostolic Succession as related to all these matters'. The Special Committee was set up by the General Assembly of 1960 to discuss these four subjects with the Anglicans and to report the result of their discussions to the General Assembly. At the request of the Anglicans the 1963 General Assembly extended the remit of the Special Committee. It did so in the following words: 'The General Assembly . . . approved the inclusion of the three additional questions, namely, the Church as Royal Priesthood, the Place of the Laity in the Church, and the Relations between Church, State and Society, as arising out of and relevant to the discussion of the four previous questions remitted to the Special Committee'. (Assembly Reports 1963, p.90).

There was thus never any doubt about the orders which the General Assembly gave to the Special Committee. These orders were to discuss four (later seven) abstract subjects. They did not include any permission to bring forward proposals for a union between the Church of Scotland and any Anglican Church. The Holland House Affair was the attempt made by the Ecumenical majority on the Special Committee to disobey the orders of the General Assemblies of 1960, 1963 and 1965 and to bring specific concrete proposals for a union with the Scottish Episcopal Church before the General Assembly of 1966.

It is obvious that any account of the plot must be as well documented as possible. One obvious source is the published report, *The Anglican-Presbyterian Conversations*.[1] This report is the official report of the conversations and it was published in March 1966 by those who took part in them, the committees of the four churches. We will accordingly refer to it as the Official Report. In addition reports, which have not been published, were submitted to the Holland House Conference by the various Regional Groups. These Regional Groups were formed to save travel expense. Originally there were four of these, the London Group, the North of England Group, and the Edinburgh Group and the Glasgow Group. Each of them consisted of a selection of committee members from the four

1. Published by the S.P.C.K. and St. Andrew Press.

churches, each of them discussed the seven subjects laid down for discussion[1] and each of them sent up a report to the Holland House Conference.

There was a fifth group, which came to be known as the Scottish Regional Group. It was formed later than the other groups. Its first meeting was in June 1965. In consisted of 18 members drawn from the Special Committee (about 14 of whom might be considered to have fairly pronounced Ecumenical views) and the whole 15 of the Scottish Episcopal committee which was taking part in the Conversations. It had no English Presbyterian or Church of England members.

The official report, *The Anglican-Presbyterian Conversations*, though prepared subsequently to the Holland House Affair, is not satisfactory as a source for that affair. It is helpful in describing the setting up of the Scottish Regional Group (except that in describing the authorisation of the formation of this Group by the 1965 General Assembly, it departs from the exact words of the Assembly). Its account of the dates on which the Scottish Regional Group met differs from that given in the Group's own report. It says that a full day meeting took place in November whereas the Scottish Regional Group's report talks of a meeting on 29th October. Since on that day all the Kirk members of the Scottish Regional Group were involved in a Special Committee meeting at 10 a.m. any meeting of the Regional Group which took place thereafter could not have been a full-day one. Further, the Official Account says that the Scottish Regional Group tentatively discussed the idea of a Binding Covenant. It does not tell that this was the only subject which the Group discussed or that the scheme was a quite specific one with a date attached to it. It does not mention the Report which the Scottish Regional Group, like the other Regional Groups, prepared for the Holland House Conference. Nor does the Official Report give any account of what the Special Committee did when the Scottish Regional Group's Report, the Grey Document, was transmitted to it. It follows that anyone relying solely on the Official Report would not

1. To be more precise, six of these subjects. The seventh, Church Community and Society was reserved for a Special Group.

know what the Holland House Affair was or even that there had been such a thing. He might very well go away with the impression that the whole thing had been invented by the *Scottish Daily Express*. As one of the purposes of this book is to enable the reader to decide whether attacks made on the *Scottish Daily Express* specifically in the Convocation of Canterbury and on the Press generally in the General Assembly were justified, it is therefore necessary to draw on other sources, which ought to be among other material in the Appendix at the end of this chapter. These are the Grey Document itself and the relevant minutes of the Special Committee which were confidential during the lifetime of that Committee. Both of these were in the possession of Dr. Dougall when he criticised the Press in the 1966 General Assembly. When Dr. Tomkins attacked the *Scottish Daily Express*, he may well not have had the minutes of the Special Committee of which, of course, he was not a member. But as convener of the corresponding Church of England Committee, he is bound to have known of its decisions with regard to the Grey Document. And like all who had been present at Holland House, he had the Grey Document in his possession.

Having then dealt with the question of sources, let us now try and draw from them an account of what happened. Chronologically the first incident seems to have been that one of the original four Regional Groups, the Glasgow Regional Group, went beyond discussion of the seven subjects laid down by the Assembly. Here is what the Official Report says:

'There has come from one Regional Group the suggestion that it should be possible to enter a United Church which would be conciliar (presbyteral and episcopal), in which existing ministries were mutually recognized. All future ordinations would be episcopal-presbyteral and within the succession hitherto formally acknowledged by the Churches of the Anglican Communion. The rights and convictions of congregations would be fully respected, for example in the appointment of ministers. This is at present no more than a suggestion:'[1]

1. The Anglican Presbyterian Conversations, p. 28.

This is, of course, quite a suggestion. Translated out of Ecumenical language, it is the suggestion that all future Church of Scotland ministers must be ordained by an Anglican Bishop. But if, as the Official Report says, it is a mere suggestion, the indication of a line of approach which might be followed in future Anglican-Presbyterian conversations, no sensible person would make a fuss about the Glasgow Group departing from the Assembly's instructions on this single occasion.

What the Official Report does not say is that the suggestion was not allowed to remain a mere suggestion. Nor does it mention that no one seems to have been disposed to leave it to future conversations but that in the current Dougall-Tomkins ones a brand new Regional Group was set up, whose report indicates that its sole purpose was to follow up and make as specific as possible the mere suggestion of the Glasgow Group.

There is a certain obscurity about the genesis of this new Scottish Regional Group but presumably there was some sort of liaison between the Scottish Episcopal leaders and the Ecumenicals on the Special Committee. The Official Report credits the Scottish Regional Group to the Scottish Episcopal Bishops, the Scottish Regional Group ascribes it to the inspiration of the Scottish Episcopal Primus. Both these documents note that the Scottish Regional Group had the authorisation of the General Assembly of 1965. The Official Report's account of this authorisation is imprecise, that given by the report of the Scottish Regional Group (The Grey Document) is quite untrue. The former account is that the suggestion of 'direct discussion between the two Scottish Churches within the framework of the current four-Church conversations . . . was noted with approval by the General Assembly in May 1965'.[1] The latter is 'The Scottish Regional Group . . . was set up to continue discussion within the framework of the present conversations after the regional groups instituted in 1962 had completed their review of the seven topics given to them. This action received the approval of . . . the General Assembly of the Church of Scotland at its meeting in May 1965'. What the Assembly of 1965 actually did was to authorise the discussions of the Scottish

1. The Anglican Presbyterian Conversations, p. 9.

Regional Group 'within the framework of the present remit given by the General Assembly to the Special Committee'.[1] The General Assembly of 1965 explicitly confined the discussions of the Scottish Regional Group to the seven subjects laid down by the Assemblies of 1960 and 1963.

It is impossible to conceive that the exact terms of their remit from the Assembly of 1965 were unknown to the Convener and Secretary of the Special Committee and to all the other 16 members of the Special Committee who had served on the Scottish Regional Group. Yet before a month was up the Assembly's instructions were being disobeyed in the Scottish Regional Group. The report of that Group, the Grey Document, shows that the Group never made the slightest pretence of discussing the seven subjects it was told to discuss by the Assembly.

What it did was to take the Glasgow Regional Group's plan for episcopal ordination of all future Church of Scotland ministers and join this to the Nottingham Conference's idea of a Binding Covenant and a date for the one Church. The result of the Scottish Regional Group's deliberations was to put forward the concrete proposal that the Church of Scotland bind itself in a Covenant to unite with the Scottish Episcopal Church under bishops in fifteen years time. This pledge, once it went through the Assembly, was irrevocable, there was to be no going back. In the meantime any new Church of Scotland ministers were to be ordained by Scottish Episcopal bishops.

One feature of the Scottish Regional Group's work may well escape those unversed in Ecumenical language. It modified the 'mere suggestion' of the Glasgow Regional Group in the interests of the Scottish Episcopal Church delegates. The latter in return for being allowed to ordain all future Church of Scotland ministers were not after all to be asked to recognise present Church of Scotland ministers as real ministers. They had simply to 'accept' them, presumably in the same way as one accepts rheumatism or old age.

There is reason to believe that the Church of Scotland members of the Scottish Regional Group were aware of the

1. Assembly Reports, 1965.

improper nature of their conduct in bringing forward a concrete scheme of union with the Scottish Episcopal Church. Readers of the Minute of the Meeting of the Special Committee on 29th October 1965 will see that at ten o'clock on that morning and therefore presumably before the meeting of the Scottish Regional Group, they were trying out the plan later to be embodied in the Report of the Scottish Regional Group. The result was evidently deemed to be satisfactory, which was not surprising in view of the fact that by this time the Ecumenical Party had a majority in the Special Committee. Having then seen how far they could go, the Kirk members of the Scottish Regional Group proceeded the same day to a meeting of that body and carried out the next stage in their plan.

This consisted in drawing up the Report of the Scottish Regional Group and sending it to the Special Committee for consideration at its meeting on 26th November. The Minute shows that when the Kirk members of the Scottish Regional Group arrived at this meeting there was a violent storm.

The non-Ecumenicals present very properly point out that the Special Committee's Assembly remit gave it no authority to entertain such proposals, that they were akin to the Craig ones rejected by the Assembly and that they arose, not from the Special Committee's own deliberations but from Nottingham resolutions which were none of its concern. To maintain the Special Committee's parentage of the proposals, the Ecumenicals claimed they were the working out of two sentences in the Glasgow Report—the very two sentences which on p.28 of the Official Report are dismissed lightly as a 'mere suggestion'.

The Ecumenical majority soon outvoted these very proper objections of the non-Ecumenicals and proceeded to make further arrangements for carrying out what the *Scottish Daily Express* has been criticised for calling the Holland House Plot. It carried a motion that the Grey Document was to be presented unaltered to the Conference, where, with the Ecumenicals reinforced by their Anglican allies, it was bound to be approved. It carried a further motion that the findings of the Conference were to be presented to the Assembly as the Special Committee's Report. At this point in the proceedings

the Ecumenicals must have felt pretty good. They had completely outwitted their ecclesiastical superiors. In spite of all
that the Assemblies of 1960 and 1965 had done to preclude this,
the Assembly of 1966 was to be presented with quite definite
concrete proposals for a union with the Scottish Episcopal
Church. It only remained to round off a successful meeting by
taking some security precautions. Members were warned that
the Press were interested in all these matters. They were told
that at the Conference they were not to speak to the Press.
Dr. Dougall and his fellow-Conveners would do that for them.

For the non-Ecumenical minority the problem of loyalty
was acute. Were they to stand by and see the Special Committee
of which they were members violate the orders of the General
Assembly from whom they had their commission? The non-
Ecumenicals tried to deal with this problem in different ways.
One of them wrote a very able memorandum pointing out the
unconstitutional nature of the Binding Covenant, the present
writer told the Special Committee's secretary that in the circumstances he could not in conscience attend the Holland
House Conference. These protests were futile. One step was
taken which was not futile. A copy of the Grey Document was
put into the hands of the *Daily Express.*

Looking back, one can see that on the 26th November the
Ecumenicals overplayed their hand. Confident that the Spirit
of God was leading them on and that they now had a safe
majority on the Special Committee, they did not notice that
they had put their opponents in a desperate position. The non-
Ecumenicals on the Special Committee were being called upon
silently to acquiesce in a plot against the authority of the
General Assembly which, if successful, would mean that for
them secession from the Church of Scotland was inevitable and
could not be long delayed. The message of the Grey Document
had been underlined by its compilers. 'The Covenant' it ran
*'must express the passing of the point of no return for both Churches:
we are committed, and committed irrevocably.'* (Italics are in the Grey
Document.)

Once that point was reached there was no longer any place
for the non-Ecumenical in the Church of Scotland.

There is no evidence that, faced with what the Germans call a boundary situation, the non-Ecumenical members of the Special Committee took any cohesive step as a group. But as individuals they may in their extremity have consulted one or two members of the Church of Scotland known to be unable for conscientious reasons to remain in it should an Anglican take-over bid as outlined in the Grey Document succeed. To this category belongs Mr. Ian McColl, the Editor of the *Scottish Daily Express*. To those who ascribe every action of that journal to the shades of the late Lord Beaverbrook, it may come as a surprise to know that the present Editor is an elder, a session clerk and a member of the Presbytery of Glasgow. He can in fact be found in that court of the Kirk, helping to transact some of its rather dull routine business on some of these occasions when its more notable Ecumenical party leaders are absent.

The scene was now finally set for the Holland House Affair and its exposure. In the early hours of the morning of 5th January, when the Church of England delegates were already travelling northward and the Grey Document lay in Holland House among the papers to be dealt with at the Conference, the *Scottish Daily Express* published an outline of its contents. This outline is printed in the Appendix to this Chapter.

It was necessary to do this for two reasons. Firstly, those Ecumenicals who criticise the *Scottish Daily Express* boast that they never read it and this curiously *a priori* attitude may impress other non-readers of that journal. Secondly, in March in the Convocation of Canterbury the Bishop of Bristol launched an attack of quite extraordinary violence on the *Scottish Daily Express*. In May at the General Assembly, Dr. Dougall, in reply to a question, cast reflections on the accuracy of the press accounts of the Holland House Conference. Neither of these gentlemen supplied any evidence for his attack.

Appendix to Chapter 16

EXTRACT FROM THE SCOTTISH DAILY EXPRESS
WEDNESDAY 5TH JANUARY 1966

'More than 120 delegates from the Kirk, the Presbyterian Church of England, the Church of England, and the Scottish Episcopal Church will meet in private in Holland House, one of Edinburgh University's Halls of Residence.

The result of the deliberations will be revealed on Friday. Before then a small but powerful group of Scottish Churchmen, hope to complete a scheme for what will be known as a 'Covenant of Union.'

Stripped of ecclesiastical verbiage, here are this group's shock hopes.

1 THAT the Church of Scotland will unite, under bishops, with the Scottish Episcopalians (and this "Covenant" is likely to be proposed by one of the Episcopal group).

2 THAT this decision, having been agreed (they hope) by the General Assembly and the Episcopal Convocation, shall be irrevocable.

3 THAT no more Kirk ministers shall be ordained, except in the presence of a bishop.

What do the Episcopalians offer in return for this total surrender of Presbyterian principles? (In italics in *Express*.)

1 They will recognise existing Church of Scotland ministers — until such time as they are all dead.

2 They will no longer forbid their flock to take Communion in the Church of Scotland."

17

Aftermath of Holland House

The first reaction of the morning of January 5th came from the *Glasgow Herald*. A representative of that paper had read an early edition of the *Scottish Daily Express* and contacted some of those taking part in the Holland House Conference in order to seek confirmation or denial of the disclosures made in the *Express*. As a result of his investigations the *Glasgow Herald* published on the same morning of the 5th January an article headed, 'Bishops Proposal Denied'. This article contained the following statements.

'Delegates to a three-day conference on Church unity which opens in Edinburgh to-day said last night that they knew of no proposal to introduce bishops into a suggested united Church formed by the Church of Scotland and the Episcopal Church in Scotland.

A report suggested that under the proposal no Church of Scotland ministers would be ordained except in the presence of a bishop and Episcopalians would no longer be forbidden to take communion in the Church of Scotland. . . .

Last night the . . . secretary of the Church of Scotland's Special Committee on Anglican-Presbyterian Relations said the conference would be discussing a number of points but he did not know of anybody making a specific proposal about the introduction of bishops into a united Church. Such a recommendation would have to be put to the General Assembly.

. . . a member of the Episcopal delegation said: 'I certainly could not say anything about this being a proposal that is going to be made. The conference will not be finished until Friday, when a statement will be given to the Press.'

As the brief northern January day wore on, the Conference got into its stride. It started off with a sermon from Dr. Dougall in St. Giles. In this he remarked how bad it was that Scotsmen should have more than one church when in their lands beyond the sea, young Christians had only one. There have been occasional rumours that some at least of Dr Dougall's young Christians are not averse to having two wives in the vicarage, in which case Scotsmen with their monogamous manses might face them without a blush. This naturally is a point which Dr. Dougall did not take up. His sermon is also reported on the testimony of Dr. Whitley, a partisan if sensitive witness, to have contained an attack on St. Giles, the church whose hospitality he was enjoying.

The devotional part of the proceedings thus concluded, the four conveners met for an hour and, in spite of the morning's denial proceeded to make an admission. The actual words of this are important. They run:

'A confidential report from one of the four regional groups took up the question of how a united church in Scotland could incorporate both Presbyteral and Episcopal systems.

This was also discussed in the Scottish Regional Group, whose unfinished report, among many other papers, comes to the Conference for discussion.'

A church which incorporates Presbyteral and Episcopal systems is Ecumenical jargon for a church where presbyteries are not actually abolished but where there are bishops. That a proposal to bring about such a church existed was exactly what the *Glasgow Herald* had in all good faith published a denial of that same morning. This denial followed by an admission was a shattering blow to the Ecumenicals' constant claim to be inspired by the Holy Spirit. Newspapermen may be irreverent but they, at anyrate, are not irreverent enough to believe that the Holy Spirit misleads the Press.

Even apart from this major point of content, the form of words of the Conveners' admission is important. First place is given to what the Official Report was later to describe as the 'mere suggestion' of two sentences tucked away in the Glasgow

Regional Group report, which in the rest of its material confines itself to the subjects authorised by the Assembly. The really hot document, the report of the Scottish Regional Group, which produced the furore at the November 26th meeting, and whose main thesis, not just two sentences, is a concrete proposal to unite not just with any episcopal church but with the Scottish Episcopal one, is quietly moved into second place. Its importance is played down. It is incomplete, one of many documents, despite the fact that it is the only one which contravenes Assembly orders and the only one which proposes a basis, the Binding Covenant, for any future talks between the two churches. Nonetheless there was on the 5th January an admission if only in Ecumenical language that there was a proposal to unite the Church of Scotland under bishops contained in the report of the Scottish Regional Group and that this report was coming to the conference for discussion. This admission by the four Conveners is interesting in the light of subsequent statements by two of them, Dr. Dougall and Dr. Tomkins. It was made after deliberation of only one hour in the face of the emergency caused by the *Scottish Daily Express*'s publication of the contents of the report of the Scottish Regional Group. It could be inconsistent with the policy which they adopted on maturer consideration of the situation and which bore fruit in the happenings of January to May 1966. To this we must now turn.

The *Scottish Daily Express*'s publication of the terms of the Grey Document impaled the Ecumenical party on the horns of an exceedingly painful dilemma. Either they had at Holland House, and in the Special Committee's Deliverance to the 1966 General Assembly, to move that the Church of Scotland enter into new discussions with the Scottish Episcopal Church with a view to union on the basis of a Binding Covenant. But if they did that, they had to give up accusing the *Scottish Daily Express* of distorting news and for years the *Scottish Daily Express* had had a place in Ecumenical mythology not unlike that of the Jews in the Nazi mythology. Or else they could regretfully put the Binding Covenant into cold storage for a more convenient occasion and in the meantime get on with the job of attacking the *Scottish Daily Express*.

The first alternative was, of course, the original plan which obviously would have been put into operation if the *Scottish Daily Express* had not disclosed it prematurely. Indeed, as late as a post-Holland House meeting of the Special Committee on 26th January a very distinguished Ecumenical party leader was urging that a variant of it should be put into operation. It certainly must have been maddening to abandon such a cleverly conceived plan. If, as is likely, the Ecumenicals either deny that there was a Holland House affair or ascribe everything they did to the Holy Spirit, they will be doing scant justice to their own ingenuity in concocting the plan. One does not fully appreciate the Holland House affair if one merely looks at it, as we have hitherto done, as an attempt to evade the orders of the Assemblies of 1960 and 1965. For it was a way of dealing with future Assemblies as well as past ones. The scheme outlined in the Grey Document was that the '*suggested basis for future discussion* (italics those of the Grey Document) between the Church of Scotland and the Scottish Episcopal Church' should be the statement 'that the two churches should publicly enter into a binding covenant to work for a united Church, which would include both Episcopalian and Presbyterian essentials, and that as an earnest of their sincerity in this commitment they would, from the time of the binding covenant, accept each other's ministries and welcome each other's communicants as a means of growing into organic unity.' If the 1966 Assembly could be brought to accept discussions on this basis— and at the time the Holland House affair was framed there were good hopes of an Ecumenical party majority in the 1966 Assembly—the Ecumenicals would have won their decisive victory. Constitutionally, in view of the Barrier Act, the Church of Scotland would not have been committed to the Binding Covenant. But morally, it would have been very difficult to get out of it. Any speaker in any post-1966 Assembly who proposed to depart from the Binding Covenant would have been accused of breaking faith with the Scottish Episcopal Church. The Kirk would have been quite firmly caught in the Anglican web.

Exasperating though it must have been to have to turn back on the very brink of success, all the signs are that cautious counsels prevailed and the second alternative was adopted. The *Official Report, The Anglican-Presbyterian Conversations,* seems to give this impression. We have seen how it describes the Glasgow Regional Group's proposal for episcopal ordination of future Kirk ministers as 'a mere suggestion' for future talks and fails to mention that a new Regional Group was formed for no other apparent reason than to turn the 'mere suggestion' into a concrete plan to be submitted to the Holland House Conference. The Binding Covenant is also played down in the Official Report. The relevant passage is on pages 1 and 2. 'The Scottish Regional Group has tentatively discussed the idea of [a binding covenant to work for a united Church, which would include both Presbyterian and Episcopalian essentials, and that as an earnest of their sincerity in this commitment the Churches would, from the time of the binding covenant, accept each other's ministries and welcome each other's communicants as a means of growing into organic unity].' The words in square brackets are, of course, taken from the Grey Document. In the Official Report they are followed by a sentence which begins, 'Without expressing any view on this tentative formulation of the idea . . .' But in the actual Grey Document these identical words are allowed by the sentence, 'This meeting (on October 29th) agreed that the statement just quoted should be taken as a *suggested basis for future discussion* (italics those of the Grey Document) between the Church of Scotland and Scottish Episcopal Church should they decide on more formal conversations.' As the Special Committee was going to press the General Assembly for just such formal conversations, the Binding Covenant had a pretty specific place in its scheme of things. But in the Official Report the Binding Covenant becomes an idea tentatively formulated just as the two sentences in the Glasgow Regional Group report which had led to the setting up of the Scottish Regional Group become a mere suggestion. The upshot is that anyone reading the Official Report will get the impression that the *Scottish Daily Express* was making a great deal of fuss about very little. One cannot, of course, prove that the Official Report gives this impression of the *Scottish Daily Express* deliberately or just through intentional inaccuracies.

There was, however, nothing unintentional about the next set of attacks which were launched against the *Scottish Daily Express*. These were extremely interesting for they mark the first occasion on which the English bishops came out openly in support of the men who were carrying out their policy in the Church of Scotland. No doubt this was felt to be necessary because of the way in which the *Scottish Daily Express*'s exposure of the Grey Document had dented the Ecumenical image. At the end of the Holland House Conference, for instance, both the *Scotsman* and the *Glasgow Herald* were openly critical of the Ecumenical party policy. At anyrate the English bishops now found it necessary to comment on the Scottish scene. On two occasions between the Holland House Conference and the General Assembly, the *Scottish Daily Express* was able to report the pounding it was taking from the historic episcopate. Both the bishops concerned had been at the Holland House Conference and both were consequently in possession of the Grey Document, and, presumably, since they were attacking it, of the *Scottish Daily Express*'s account of that document.

First came Dr. Easthaugh, Bishop of Peterborough. The *Scottish Daily Express* quoted an extract from his Diocesan leaflet of which the following is part.

'During the conference the *Scottish Daily Express* shamelessly exploited this emotional factor in a persistent campaign to discredit the conversations. Presbyterian divines were branded as "traitors" in large headlines for discussing the possibility of taking Episcopacy into the Presbyterian system. And Anglican bishops were described as sinister plotters attempting to disrupt the Scottish Kirk. All this was calculated to arouse Scottish fears and animosity and to inhibit the rational, to say nothing of the Christian, discussion of the fundamental mission and pattern of a united Christian church. One can only hope that in the virulence of this campaign the *Scottish Daily Express* has over-reached itself. But it provides a classic instance of the way psychological and emotional factors can be used to defeat the purpose of God. Prejudice is too respectable a word to use for this sort of thing because it implies some attempt at rational judgment—a very different thing from emotional reaction.'

Even more violent was the salvo fired by Dr. Tomkins, Bishop of Bristol, during the Convocation of Canterbury. Talking of 'the tyrannous pretensions of this strident spokesman of the Fourth Estate', he blamed the *Scottish Daily Express* for the rejection of the Craig Report and went on to say:

'The Scottish edition of a popular daily newspaper vitiated all discussion, and still does, by shrill vituperation and gross distortion.'[1]

After this prodigious barrage from the English episcopate it is not surprising that Ecumenical party speakers were emboldened to attack the Press in the General Assembly. Here the key passage is a dialogue between the Rev. George Dale and Dr. Dougall. Mr. Dale asked why it had been first denied and then admitted 'that a plan for union between the Kirk and the Scottish Episcopal Church providing for the Episcopal ordination of all future Church of Scotland ministers was being put forward to the Holland House Conference.' To this Dr. Dougall's reply was, 'That illustrates the danger of taking the daily Press as a guide rather than the reports of the actual conversations. There was never any proposal of any such kind discussed.'

The evidence seems to show that Dr. Dougall's attack on the Press paid off. It was echoed by a Mr. Gibson of Rutherglen. Dr. Dougall's deliverance with a supporting addendum by Mr. Gibson was carried by 23 votes and Dr. Dougall and three of the other members of the Scottish Regional Group which produced the Grey Document were elected to the new committee to open conversations with the Scottish Episcopal Church. It could well be that Dr. Dougall's narrow but decisive majority was won because of his statement that his Special Committee had suffered because of inaccurate Press reports.

The policy of abandoning the Binding Covenant and attacking the *Scottish Daily Express* (though Dr. Dougall, unlike the English bishops, does not mention that journal by name) was thus a victory for the Anglicans and their fellow travellers, and therefore, in Ecumenical language, a victory for the Will of God. The Binding Covenant need only be dropped temporarily and

1. This outburst by the Bishop of Bristol was replied to in a very dignified and restrained article by Mr Charles Graham in the *Scottish Daily Express*.

indeed, only a few months after the Assembly, a Scottish Episcopal Bishop was finding it the outstanding feature of the Official Report.

But success in ecclesiastical politics is not the only criterion of action and one or two troublesome issues arise out of the post-Holland House Ecumenical campaign. The Bishop of Peterborough's attack on the *Scottish Daily Express* is just what we have found to be the age old ecclesiastical gambit for getting your own way by identifying it with the purpose of God. Having thus established that the people opposing his plan are against God, the Bishop makes the traditional second move of giving them hell. 'Prejudice is too respectable a word to use for this sort of thing because it implies some attempt at rational judgment—a very different thing from emotional reaction.' Just in case the *Scottish Daily Express* is feeling happy about itself the Bishop of Bristol joins in and says, 'it vitiated all discussion and still vitiates it by shrill vituperation'.

These statements of the two bishops are an attack presumably not on the accuracy of the *Scottish Daily Express*'s reporting but on the views which it expresses on Ecumenical matters. Now any newspaper expects criticism of its views. But to have any weight criticism must be reasoned refutation. The *Scottish Daily Express*, for instance, had said that Anglican diplomats, while professing zeal for better relations between churches were going to make it impossible for Scottish Methodists to receive Communion from Church of Scotland ministers. If the two bishops had brought forward disproof of that statement they would have been offering reasonable criticism of that journal. But they do not disprove that or any of the *Scottish Daily Express*'s other criticisms of Anglican diplomacy. Instead they simply bring against it what looks uncommonly like mere abuse. This is quite serious. If bishops cannot supply reasoned criticism but only abuse, what has the Church of Scotland to gain by taking bishops into its system?

Even more serious is a point apparently raised by the last two words of Dr. Tomkins' attack and certainly by Dr. Dougall's Assembly reply to Mr. Dale. Criticising the views of a newspaper is one thing, criticising the accuracy of its reporting is another and much more serious one. Newspapers exist to tell people the truth. To say that a newspaper (whether it be the *Times* or the *News of the World* is immaterial) is not telling the truth when in fact it is, is quite a serious matter. If such a statement is made in a high ecclesiastical court such as the Convocation of Canterbury or the General Assembly, the moral authority of such a court makes the statement all the more serious. The Church has a responsibility to the Press and this responsibility cannot be evaded by any number of protestations of enthusiasm for the Will of God.

When Dr. Tomkins attacked the *Scottish Daily Express* in the Convocation of Canterbury, was he criticising its views or the accuracy of its reporting? His use of the words 'gross distortion' suggests that he was doing the second and not just the first of these things. But it does not prove it. He may only have been meaning that the *Scottish Daily Express* was distorting the issues and not the facts. If so, the use of the word 'distortion' at a time when the main question was whether the *Scottish Daily Express* had accurately reproduced the contents of the Grey Document — a question which Dr. Tomkins was in an excellent position to answer—can only be described as unfortunate.

This brings us to Dr. Dougall's Assembly reply, which, as we have seen, could well have been a decisive statement in an Assembly debate of high policy. According to the *Glasgow Herald*, Dr. Dougall began his reply by saying 'That illustrates the danger of taking the daily press as a guide rather than the reports of the actual conversations.' This is clearly a criticism of the accuracy of the Press. It is not a criticism of the *Scottish Daily Express* specifically, though that paper must have been uppermost in the minds of Dr. Dougall's Assembly hearers. He is asserting that the Press is less accurate than the Special Committee's own reports. But in this chapter and the last we have shown that it is difficult to get the Special Committee's Official Report to tally with the reports of its Regional Groups on some quite vital points. It is therefore difficult to understand why Dr. Dougall should appear to be stressing the superior accuracy of the Official Report to that of the Press. But this difficulty pales in comparison with that aroused by Dr.

Dougall's next statement. Mr. Dale had asked about a 'plan for union between the Kirk and the Scottish Episcopal Church providing for the Episcopal ordination of all future Church of Scotland ministers'. He had asked why such a plan had been first denied and then admitted. To this Dr. Dougall replied flatly, 'There was never any proposal of any such kind discussed.' Now the report of the Glasgow Regional Group contains the statement, 'Eventually complete agreement was reached that it should be possible to enter a United Church which would be conciliar (Presbyteral and episcopal), in which existing ministries were mutually recognised. All future ordinations would be episcopal-presbyteral and within the succession hitherto formally acknowledged by the Churches of the Anglican Communion.' This statement is in fact quoted on p. 28 of the Official Report. Why therefore Dr. Dougall, who a moment before had been extolling the superior accuracy of the Official Report should say that a proposal of the kind mentioned by Mr. Dale had never been discussed is inexplicable. What is disquieting is that a statement so inexplicable may well have gained the Ecumenical party its narrow margin in a debate whose outcome committed the Church of Scotland to a round of talks with the Scottish Episcopal Church.

18

The Tirrell Case

T HE events which arose in connection with the presence in 1965 and 1966 of an Episcopal priest as assistant minister in St. Giles, the High Kirk of Edinburgh, form a copybook case of an ecumenical incident. For that reason it is best to approach the whole matter as dispassionately as possible. The real agents are not the personalities involved but Ecumenical conceptions with which the earlier chapters of this book have made us familiar. It is, for instance, a pity if the character of the Edinburgh Scottish Episcopal bishop, Kenneth Carey, has been highlighted both by his critics and by his enthusiastic admirers. One must be fair to him and agree that his conduct simply displayed the same magnificent dedication to Anglican interests and aspirations which one would expect from any Anglican bishop apart from an odd unpolitical one like Bishop Pike of California. An emotional reaction to him on the part of critic or admirer only helped to exacerbate the acrimony and misery which the Ecumenical categories of the Will of God and the One church inevitably produce when they are applied to a concrete situation.

The situation arose out of different interpretations being given to the oneness extolled by the Ecumenical Movement. Harry Whitley, the minister of the High Kirk of Edinburgh and John Tirrell, the young American Episcopal curate, were naïve enough to believe that this oneness would be expressed by Presbyterians and Episcopalians loving one another and manifesting their love by coming together to the Lord's Table.

This, of course, is entirely to ignore the claim to exclusiveness and the power drives, which, as we saw in Chapter 6, also find expression in oneness. If Tirrell, an episcopally ordained priest, were in St. Giles to offer communion to non-episcopally confirmed Presbyterians he would cease to be upholding the Anglican communion's claim to be part of the One Church in the sense in which the Church of Scotland is not. Further, by so doing, he would be offering Church of Scotland members intercommunion without first exacting the requirement that they accept union with the Scottish Episcopal Church under bishops. This would be fatal to any plan for getting a million-strong church on the northern border of England under the control of Anglican consecrated bishops.

It was thus inevitable that Tirrell's sacramental ministry in St. Giles should be stopped by action from the Anglican side. The way this action was received again throws interesting light on factors which run right through the Ecumenical Movement. On the Anglican side, Bishop Carey's action in inhibiting Mr. Tirrell met with virtually complete support. Whatever was felt, nothing was said openly in criticism of Carey or done to make his position more difficult. This is where one takes off one's hat to Anglicans. Like all Englishmen, they are loyal to their own side. Limeys don't rat, they leave it to the other side to do that. That is a slightly crisp way of putting a proposition which is basic to the understanding of the Ecumenical Movement. Whether the English really respect those on the other side who lack loyalty, or whether they simply use them is an interesting question which the non-Englishman cannot presume to answer.

On the Church of Scotland side the reaction was very different. In one of its debates on the matter the Presbytery of Edinburgh split even and all through, Whitley was subjected to a rain of criticism from within his own church such as Carey was completely spared. Nor can we be entirely sure that Whitley's opponents within the Kirk stopped at criticism. There is written evidence that one of the best known members of the Kirk's Ecumenical party saw the wretched Bishop Pike in Cambridge and it is too great a strain on the imagination to suppose that their interview was taken up with this gentleman telling the bishop the merits of Harry Whitley. Certainly

Bishop Pike was prevailed upon to withdraw his consent to Mr. Tirrell's sacramental ministry in St. Giles and in the circumstances it is impossible to exclude the possibility that representations from within the Church of Scotland played a part in making him reverse his decision.

Loyalty towards the interests of the Anglican Church and disloyalty towards those of the other church are perhaps a permanent feature of all negotiations carried out under the auspices of the Ecumenical Movement. In the Tirrell case two circumstances render this feature more interesting than usual. The first is that, viewed simply by standards prevailing in the Church of Scotland, Bishop Carey's sentence on Mr. Tirrell is so severe as to be savage. To exclude someone from taking services in all the churches of a single area in Scotland is an exercise of ecclesiastical power which simply would not be entrusted to the hands of a single man in the Church of Scotland. That it should be enforced against someone guilty only of a breach of ecclesiastical protocol is quite unthinkable within that church. Yet quite a large number of Church of Scotland ministers, particularly in Edinburgh, supported Carey and not Whitley. The interesting nature of this phenomenon is heightened by another factor. Nobody is going to question that Bishop Carey has lived a blameless and no doubt meritorious life. As a supporter of the Ecumenical Movement he has expressed his enthusiasm for the Will of God and he is on excellent terms with titled and other members of the Edinburgh establishment. As such he can appeal to both the pious and the social aspirations of Edinburgh Church of Scotland ministers. It is no disrespect to him whatever to say that he does not project the image of an exciting twentieth-century Christian ministry in the way Dr. Whitley does. Harry Whitley is, after all, known as the man who has fought for the underdog, for the downtown Glasgow housewife who found great rats basking in her kitchen sink, for the child dying helplessly of T.B. in a single end, for the soldier home from the Korean War with no place to take his bride. Carried out successfully, as Whitley carried them out, these activities no doubt produce the qualities of bluntness and plain speaking essential to anyone who is going to help the underdog by piercing through a screen of secretaries and underlings in the Kafka-like castle of bureaucracy. But as Christian activities they are perhaps a little more positive than coming down heavily on the head of an erring curate. That nonetheless they should fail to secure Dr. Whitley the support of quite a large number of his fellow Church of Scotland ministers in Edinburgh is perhaps quite an interesting example of how Ecumenical considerations affect people's sense of values.

There are one or two other interesting elements in connection with the Tirrell case. One of them is raised by Canon Montefiore. He is the honest broker who intervened in this distateful affair (the adjectives are his own). His letter describing how he introduced a leader of the Kirk's Ecumenical party to Bishop Pike in Cambridge ends with words which he was later to echo in the Convocation of Canterbury.

'Tirrell's statements and your (his correspondent's) cuttings show a dependence on the *Scottish Daily Express* that is incomprehensible to us Southerners. When the Duke of Edinburgh called the *Daily Express* "a bloody awful newspaper" he endeared himself to many of us in the South. To us it appears (I hope we are quite wrong) that the Kirk does not or dare not go against the policy of the *Scottish Daily Express*, which keeps its large circulation by playing on nationalist sentiments rather than religious conviction.'[1]

We applaud the patriotic zeal of the spunky Canon which leads him to find expression for his violent feelings in the salty language of the Royal mariner. But when the Canon on the strength of a single hasty exclamation continues to pressgang the Duke into the ranks of those hostile to the one anti-Ecumenical party paper not just in a letter but in all the publicity of the Convocation of Canterbury, then laudable enthusiasm becomes a diplomatic *gaffe* of the first order. Surely even the most fervent of Anglican imperialists is able to be sensitive to

1. The *Scottish Daily Express* (12th May 1966) reported Canon Montefiore as saying in the Convocation of Canterbury, (The Tirrell case) 'has become a *cause celebre* in Scotland—chiefly owing to the violent tone of the *Scottish Daily Express*... The influence of the *Scottish Daily Express* on the Church in Scotland seems to us who would perhaps agree with His Royal Highness' opinion of that newspaper, as very great indeed'.

the delicate position of the Royal family in matters ecumenical. Containing within their number those who have made sacrificial decisions to adhere to what is the Church of England's but not the Church of Scotland's view of marriage and divorce, related by marriage to some of the leading Scottish Episcopal families and having as their head a monarch who on her accession pledged herself to maintain the Presbyterian form of religion in Scotland, the Royal family has to stay out of the controversy about bishops in the Kirk and must be protected from even the slightest suggestion that it is doing anything else. No doubt Canon Montefiore did not intend to convey any such suggestion but even so his remark was gratuitous. Anglicans and Kirk Ecumenicals have on occasion been not averse to hinting, with various degrees of delicacy, that God was against the *Daily Express*. It was hardly necessary to bring in the Duke of Edinburgh as well.

The Tirrell case is typical of Ecumenical incidents in its production of acrimony, lovelessness and misery. The real culprits are the Ecumenical ideas themselves. Certainly we must rise above personalities and partisanship. No doubt Kenneth Carey suffered during the Tirrell case just as James Pitt-Watson and Archibald Craig suffered during the Bishops' Report controversy. But inevitably it is the other side which is bound to suffer most. For in this ghastly internecine strife among Christians which the Ecumenical Movement has brought about, it is only the Ecumenical who knows how to hallow acrimony, only he can justify any barb, however vicious, in his knowledge that it is directed against those who are opposing Christ. Certainly one only needs to read a few of the vituperative letters received by Harry Whitley to reflect that if this sort of thing is a healing of the body of Christ, then Donnybrook Fair is a health centre and the Kilkenny cats are medical practitioners.

It was, of course, absurd of Dr. Whitley to think that he could attack Anglican imperialism and retain the favour of the Establishment of Edinburgh, that curious city where for so many years the passport to social success was the possession of an English accent. It may be that he never gave this matter a thought, but in any case the Establishment will know how to deal with him. It will deal with him as all Establishments deal with those who do not conform, by the social death of a thousand pinpricks. What will happen to him will be a succession of slights so slight as to make him wonder if they really are slights at all and at any rate so slight that no sensible man would do anything about them. But there will be so many of them that they will affect him and eventually no doubt make him see slights where none were intended. And so the pinpricks and imagined pinpricks will multiply a thousandfold. Only occasionally will they amount to something that Dr. Whitley can deal with, an attack on St. Giles by an Ecumenical leader, the insults of a drunken nobleman, the kind of gossip that can be dealt with by a lawyer's letter.

Lastly the Tirrell case shows how little things change. In discussing it we have talked about the position of the Crown, of the Scottish nobles and of disloyal Scots. John Knox, Harry Whitley's most eminent predecessor as minister of St. Giles, would have talked of just these very things. They made up Knox's problems too. Most formidable of all for Knox as for Whitley was the drive of English imperialism. In Knox's time as we saw in Chapter 8, it was motivated by strategic necessity. In Whitley's time it is motivated by the necessity to find ecclesiastical *ersatz* for a lost world power.

So the *New Christian* is right in saying that the Tirrell case shows that we in Scotland have difficulty in getting into the twentieth century. It is wrong in attributing this to people like Harry Whitley. Harry Whitley, the Presbytery of Glasgow's authority on housing, was very much a twentieth-century figure. It is the Ecumenical Movement which has dragged him back into the sixteenth century.

PART FOUR

Anglo-Scottish Ecclesiastical Relations

The Present and the Future

19

English and Scottish Nationalism

It has been argued, e.g. by the Editor of Crockford, by Canon Montefiore in his letter on the Tirrell case[1] and by the *New Christian* that opposition to Ecumenicity in Scotland comes from Scottish Nationalism. This must a cheering conclusion for the Ecumenicals. For behind Ecumenicity in the English-speaking part of the world lies Anglicanism and imbedded in Anglicanism is an English nationalism compared to which Scottish nationalism is a quite negligible force.

Nationalism is imbedded in the structure of the Anglican church. The institutional narcissism which is a feature of Englishness is expressed in the fact that bishops in the Church of England are drawn from the institutions which Englishmen romanticise most, the public schools and the universities of Oxford and Cambridge. For others the road to the gaiters is barred.

Nationalism pervades English theology. No one in their senses and least of all the present writer wishes to disparage English theology. But if Crockford, Montefiore and the *New Christian* are going to accuse the Scottish Church of nationalism, then all the cards must be laid on the table and something must be said which hitherto German, American and Scots theologians have been too polite to say. With all its merits (and they are many) English theology has one curious and slightly comic feature, its inveterate nationalism. As so much of the work in modern theology is done by Germans, English nationalism generally expresses itself in a kind of 'gun for the Hun'

1. Quoted on p. 146

motif which runs through English theology of all shades. Let us see a few examples of this. Professor Mascall, for instance, praises Dr. Farrer's essay on the Demythologising controversy[1] as 'penetrating'. This may or may not be so. What is certain is that of the hundreds of essays written in the Demythologising debate, Dr. Farrer's is the only one which implies one's nationality has any bearing on one's approach to the debate. Here is what Dr. Farrer writes:

> 'Yet, however much the Englishman admires German profundity, he cannot see things altogether with German eyes. Indeed, one effect of reading a book like this is to be reminded how foreign the German religious attitude is to our own.'

Of the seminal influences on Dr. Robinson's theology, Dr. Mascall writes: 'It is, however, interesting to remark that they all come from the background of German Protestantism, and that they all, in different ways, represent the reaction within German Protestantism from the extreme revelationism and supernaturalism of the School of Barth, Brunner and Heim'. This is a very odd estimate of the inter-relations of continental theologians (two of the three are Swiss not German) and Barth would have something fairly strong to say if you told him that as a theologian he formed a school with Brunner and Heim. But in his main contention Dr. Mascall is right. The three main influences on the Bishop of Woolwich's best-selling book were obviously Bultmann, Bonhoeffer and Tillich. Indeed there is no stronger testimony to the seriousness with which Englishmen take their own institutions than that the views of these three eminent but un-English thinkers, which had been written in some cases twenty years before, suddenly became important because they were taken up and put together not entirely consistently by an English bishop who had been at the right school and university. But let no one accuse the Bishop of Woolwich of being un-English. In the October 1961 *Journal of Theological Studies* we find him praising Oscar Cullmann as 'one of the most stimulating, coherent, and (dare I say it?)

1. In the English edition of *Kerygma and Myth.* p. 212.

Anglican of continental theologians?' And in a review in the April 1966 issue of the same Journal, the Bishop of Woolwich shows that he can be just as good an anti-German as anyone else. In reviewing Gollwitzer's *The Existence of God as confessed by Faith*, he writes 'the discussion moves wholly within the bounds of the current German theological debate. There is parochialism here which would be incredible in any Anglo-Saxon production of comparable scholarship.' The bishop, so unkindly criticised by Dr. Mascall for having borrowed from Germans, is able to say proudly that 'as an Englishman, detached yet concerned' he wants to make two comments on Gollwitzer's book. After saying some very stinging things of Barthian theology he concludes by saying that 'it is in danger of surviving with all the inaccessible magnificence of the German *Schloss*'. This is a very powerful metaphor and one hates to ask if the Englishmen of the past were so dim that they built their mediaeval castles on accessible places. And so the comedy goes on. One is forced to something like the conclusion that an English theologian, whatever his theological standpoint, has to find expression for his nationalism in his theology.

I wish to apologise to Dr. Farrer, Professor Mascall and the Bishop of Woolwich for having been forced by what is called the ecumenical dialogue to refer to what is of course by far the weakest element in their theologies. If I have singled them out it is to show how nationalism can affect the thought of even the most eminent of English theologians. It goes without saying that they are all free from the cruder English nationalist theology which condemns a theological viewpoint simply by calling it 'Teutonic'. The latter is a very damnatory word though what it means apart from 'un-English' is hard to say.

In fairness to German theologians it must be said they do not bring nationalism into theology and do not trouble to reply to the anti-German motif in English theology. A professional theologian can hardly fail to notice the difference between an English and a German theological conference. At some point or other at an English theological conference someone is sure to start talking about German theologians and how odd they are.

At a German theological conference people do not talk about English theologians—they just talk about theology.

This nationalistic element is lacking in Scots theology, much of which has simply consisted in Scotsmen making German theology available for English and American readers.

A writer like John Baillie can refer to 'our great Archbishop, Anselm of Canterbury'. He can in his posthumous Gifford Lectures express a preference for Samuel Johnson over his contemporary David Hume. Hume, the greatest of all Scottish thinkers was a charming agnostic on excellent terms with the Presbytery of Edinburgh, and could show kindness even to the very difficult Rousseau. Johnson, the devout Anglican, was an extremely rude neurotic, and his attitude to Scotsmen was not dissimilar to a moderate twentieth century anti-semitism. If John Baillie ranks Johnson above Hume one may fairly claim that his judgment as a theologian is not swayed by nationalist factors.

In recent Scottish theology the disloyalty syndrome finds fascinating expression in G.B. Burnet's *The Holy Communion in the Reformed Church of Scotland 1560–1960*.[1] Dr. Burnet's anti-nationalist bias is so great as seriously to impair his work as a historian and theologian.

We are not, of course, entitled to fault Dr. Burnet simply for having a bias. My own bias in these matters is that I tend to assume that Scotsmen found God in the Sacrament in all ages both before and after the Reformation. Dr. Burnet's bias is best indicated on p.281, 'Few will dispute the weakness of the devotional life of the Church of Scotland today and the low spiritual category of her members in general.' Dr. Burnet is perfectly entitled to criticise the Church of Scotland and it may well be that it requires criticism. But I think we are entitled to ask if his bias ever makes his criticism unfair? I think it does when he implies that the open-air communions were occasions for sexual immorality when such a thing is not even hinted at in the work of a contemporary and not particularly friendly observer like the Author of *Peter's Letters to his Kinsfolk*. And I think it also does when he writes '. . . the Puritan tradition

1. Published by the Oxford University Press.

of the 17th and 18th centuries has tended to warp, if not un-wittingly to smother, in the minds of Scottish worshippers the conscious sense of fellowship with the Church Universal, and to create instead an atmosphere of superior denominational loyalty harmful to the spirit of unifying love to all the congrega-tion of the faithful', without once in the whole book men-tioning the invitation to partake extended to members of all branches of the Church which is a feature of the Church of Scotland Communion Service. Secondly, we are entitled to ask if this particular bias is a handicap in this particular subject matter, I think it is, as a corresponding one would be in an Anglican or a Roman Catholic giving an account of Holy Communion in his Church. Perhaps the sacrament does not easily disclose its secrets to those who are unduly censorious of the attitude of others toward it. The only times the numinous quality of the sacrament seems to come out in the whole book are first in a description of a Covenanting communion where the nearness of the participants to death makes the author for once desist from criticism, and, second, in the account of a communion service on Deeside in the early snows of winter which is not from the author's pen but from that of Queen Victoria.

In the field of theology then, the strong element of English nationalism which pervades Anglicanism has nothing to fear. Church of Scotland theology, so far from being nationalistic, is much more likely to reveal anti-nationalistic tendencies which illustrate the disloyalty syndrome that has run through Scottish life for centuries.

Nor is the fact that the Church of England (unlike the Catho-lic Church) debars from episcopal rank any not educated at English public schools and Oxford or Cambridge likely to stand in the way of an Anglican take over of the Church of Scotland. For one of the most interesting features of Scottish life is the way Scotsmen set aside not only their own nationalism but a plain regard for facts in order to enthuse over this par-ticular English behaviour pattern. It is hardly possible to imagine the Old Etonians dinner being treated by an English-man to a discourse on the superior merits of American coeducational high schools. English nationalism would forbid that. Yet some years ago the annual dinner of a leading Glasgow grammar school was treated to the following discourse by a leading Scottish industrialist:[1]

> 'One of the weaknesses of the Scottish education system was the lack of public school training such as in England, said Sir Alexander Fleck, chairman of the British Association for the Advancement of Science, in Glasgow on Saturday, when he spoke at the annual dinner of Glasgow Hillhead High School club on Saturday.
>
> 'I have to admit quite candidly that, statistically, we can get much better leaders of industry who have come up through universities provided they have preceded that with the benefits of the English public school system,' he added.
>
> The development of individual leadership was cultivated in the English public school in a way which would be worthy of study by the Scottish school system, he added.
>
> The same thing applied to a considerable degree in social leadership, apart from science. Where the humanities were concerned, however, his experience was that Oxford and Cambridge could turn out leadership ten times to one compared with the other universities of this country, including the non-residential universities in Scotland.'

One wonders if the Swiss international bankers to-day would agree with Sir Alexander (now Lord) Fleck. After all Scotland is not the only country to lack an Eton and an Oxford. Swedish, West German and American Schools and Universities are much more like Scottish Schools and Universities. And he would be a bold man who would write to-day[2] that Swedish, West German and American industry for lack of an Eton and an Oxford are in much worse care than English industry.

Scottish romanticisation of English public school education is surely one of the most extreme instances of Scottish anti-

1. Reported in the *Scotsman*.
2. These words are written on July 22nd 1966 on the day after Mr. Wilson's speech in the House of Commons introducing emergency measures to save the £.

nationalism in view of the fact that Scottish education is so normal and English education so odd. After all, it is only the English who have erected the cuckoo into a symbol of parenthood. To be fair it is not the public schools which are the worst feature of English education. It is true that these monastic institutions can hardly avoid producing misfits in the heterosexual early-dating post-1945 society which American superior power has brought about in contemporary Europe. But only at their worst have the English public schools been homosexual flagellation brothels. In the main the most damage is done by the private (or pre-public) schools. To these curious institutions (run for private profit) boys of eight are sent. Deprived prematurely of their mother's affection these wretched children, as Ian Suttie has shown[1] can hardly fail to fall victim of the psychological hazards of the supplanter complex and the taboo on tenderness. To one who has seen these children parting from their parents at a railway station the scene remains as a moving picture of human wretchedness, mitigated only by the kindness of the ticket collector to the little boys. No doubt he was too humane a man ever to consider sending his children to an orphanage.

That the English should admire a system so extraordinary can only be ascribed to an institutional narcissism in which their very strong nationalism is expressed. That the Scottish upper middle classes should admire it can only be explained by an unusually strong anti-nationalism which expresses itself in what we have called the disloyalty syndrome.

The conclusion is obvious. If the Ecumenical movement is going to be decided by a conflict of nationalisms, English nationalism is vastly stronger than Scottish Nationalism. The Anglicans will take over the Church of Scotland.

---

1. In his book *The Origins of Love and Hate.*

20

Sociological Survey

Ernst Troeltsch had a disconcerting knack of describing churches as they are and not as those who hold power in them induce theologians to say that they are. He is naturally not a popular thinker in these Ecumenical days but even so we may take a useful distinction from him. Troeltsch distinguished between a Volkskirche, which has some claim to be coextensive with the community and the kind of church which is relatively so small as to make any such claim ridiculous. The latter kind of religious body Troeltsch called the sect-type. I think this is an unfortunate phrase and I intend to call this type of religious body a minority church. I make the change because the use of the word 'sect' means that we are passing a negative value judgment on these religious bodies and that is to fail to do justice to Troeltsch's approach. The merit about Troeltsch's approach is that he does not bring value judgments to bear on churches. He sees them with the sterilised categories of the sociologist, not with the infected ones of the theologian, who the more catholic he claims to be, is the more likely to be a denominationalist ideologist thinking in the interests of some particular ecclesiastical power concentration.

It is apparently quite hopeless to expect the Ecumenical movement to work with sterilised categories of the sociologist, presumably because it has got into the hands of those who have an interest in keeping the categories infected. But there is no reason why we should not try and do so. In this chapter a Volkskirche (literally 'a people's church') and a minority church are used as statistical expressions and not as value judgments.

We are trying to be factual and not paying a compliment if we call a religious body a Volkskirche. Anybody who wants to find unkind things to say about a Volkskirche has only to read Kierkegaard. And we are trying to be factual and not being feline if we call a religious body a minority church. After all, it is surely a compliment to be put in the same category as the Quakers. On the other hand, the values may lie the other way round. Back in 1937 it was from the German Volkskirche that the Protestant opposition to Hitler came. The German minority churches, too small to be worth Nazi persecution, were in consequence rather too ready to say that all was well in the German garden.

A minority church just because it is small and does not have to number the average man among its members, can enforce a high standard among its members. The Quakers are an example in point. On the other hand, for the very same reason, the Christianity of the minority church can have a high nuttiness coefficient. It can insist for instance to its members that you are not a Christian if you smoke or take a drink or enjoy tea or coffee, a position which the good sense of the average citizen will not allow him to accept.

If we apply the statistical criteria of the sociologist to determine what is a Volkskirche, it is clear that the Scandinavian churches have the greatest claim to be this. The Church of Denmark for instance comprises all of the population of that country except for 5 per cent.[1] What membership of a Volkskirche means is not something we are concerned with here, though Kierkegaard quite clearly considered that it did not mean enough. For our purpose we may notice that we can express the matter roughly by saying that a Volkskirche is one of which the average man does not attend, a minority church is one which the non-average man attends. The Church of England is obviously a Volkskirche though its rating is not high as such churches go (the Anatomy of Britain gives it 2 million communicants out of a 45 million population).[2] The Church of

1. Facts about Denmark. p. 31. (Politikens Forlag, Copenhagen 1965.)
2. In this respect the Anatomy of Britain contrasts it unfavourably with the Church of Scotland which is 1.2 million communicants out of a population of 5 million.

Scotland comes out statistically higher though in industrial areas, Irish immigration and Papal prohibition of birth control, has meant that it faces an almost equal Catholic population. Further in North-West Scotland, the catastrophe of the Disruption and the collapse of Highland civilisation has meant that the Church of Scotland is virtually a minority church over against the dominant Free Church.

The Scottish Episcopal Church with its membership of 56,000 in a country with a five million population is a minority church, indeed all its membership could be comfortably fitted into one of Glasgow's new housing areas. One has the utmost respect for old Scottish episcopal families, but the most obvious thing about them is that there cannot be many of them. For they by no means form the total of the small Scottish Episcopal Church membership which comprises also presumably a few of the English resident in Scotland and also converts for the Church of Scotland who have joined it either from sound theological reasons or for the view widely held in Scotland that English institutions are U and Scottish institutions are non-U. There is no doubt that one function of the Scottish Episcopal Church is to represent English behaviour patterns in Scotland. Its higher clergy, the teachers at its denominational school, Glenalmond, are almost exclusively all products of English schools and universities.

This view would be widely disputed by the Scottish Episcopal Church who like to claim that they are the Church of Scotland. This claim, that Ecumenicals take seriously, is of course sociologically fatuous. The Scottish Episcopal Church is not the Church of Scotland for the sufficient reason that in most parts of Scotland Scottish Episcopalians are so thin on the ground as to be virtually non-existent. Their strength is supposed to lie in the North-East of Scotland, but the visitor to a village in that area may find the greatest evidence of their presence in a few graves in a pitifully neglected church yard.

One does not like saying these things of one's fellow Christians. It would be far better if the Episcopal Church were really strong in Scotland and did not just pretend to be. For years Church of Scotland members have been too polite to say this to them. It is a great pity this politeness cannot continue, but when the Scottish Episcopal Bishop Carey in the course of a controversy which brought pain and dissension to the Church of Scotland though not, thanks to its superior loyalty, to his own denomination, talks of 'two great churches', he makes some straight sociological talking necessary.

The real strength of the Scottish Episcopal Church lies in its class composition. By no means all the Scottish nobles belong to it. Some are Catholics, quite a number belong to the Kirk. But a number, including some who have family connections with the Royal Family, do. The amount of pressure the Episcopalians can put on that curious body the Edinburgh establishment and those Church of Scotland divines who wish to stand well with it is quite considerable as the unfortunate Dr. Whitley was to find. The winter of the Tirrell case would have been much less unpleasant for him if he had been minister of the Great Kirk of Glasgow, Aberdeen or Dundee, and not of St. Giles, Edinburgh.

No one would deny the high ethical standards of the members of the Scottish Episcopal Church and fail to acclaim their magnificent efforts to bear witness to a very real form of Christian witness in such an area as the Gorbals of Glasgow. But it would be equally unrealistic to deny that the Scottish Episcopal Church has a high nuttiness coefficient. As with so many minority churches numerical inferiority finds compensation in a superiority complex which in turn manifests itself in an exclusion policy. Like the Jehovah's Witnesses and the Close Brethren, the Scottish Episcopal Church regards Church of Scotland members as second class Christians, without proper ministers and without proper sacraments. Just as the Jehovah's Witnesses find it difficult to find a place for Kirk members in heaven and Close Brethren find it difficult to give them a place at the dinner table, so the Scottish Episcopalians find it difficult to share a place with them at the Communion Table. There is nothing very remarkable or unique about all this. The plain fact is that the burden of loving others has often been too heavy for Christians and they have only been able to bear it by finding quasi-theological reasons for looking down on other Christians. Surely the response to this very human failing is to show charity and understanding. As we shall see, the Church of Scotland tends to be tolerant towards nuttiness. As far as the present writer is concerned if it gives Scottish Episcopalians comfort to say that he is not a minister, he would be the last to deny them that comfort. But getting him to say that Bonhoeffer was not one is quite a different matter. But that would be to take us into the realm of theology and for the present we are confining ourselves to the sociologist's antiseptic weapons of statistics. If we confine ourselves to that, the present position is that the Church of Scotland, a body of a million members, is in danger of being broken in two if it will not accept *in toto* the nuttiness of 56,000 Scottish Episcopalians. One thing remains to be said to the Ecumenical party members who have controlled the Kirk's Inter-Church Relations in the last decade or two. Their activities which have brought the Church of Scotland to this pass are not diplomacy. They are simply and more accurately described as ineptitude.

On the other hand, sociologically it is obvious that union with the Church of Scotland (on their terms, of course) will bring the bishops of the Scottish Episcopal Church certain advantages. If you enjoy being called 'my Lord'—and if you dislike it you don't need to become a bishop—then you will prefer being called 'my Lord' by a million people rather than by a mere 56,000. With this go certain bonus points such as being moved from a fringe to a feature position at Edinburgh's more Ruritanian fiestas.

These social perquisites will have to wait until 1980, though that is not so far off. But if the Binding Covenant goes into operation the Scottish Episcopal bishops stand to gain an immediate bonus of power. No Church of Scotland ordination will be able to take place without one of them and this will give them a very good leverage within that Church. In terms of the power equations the Binding Covenant is sheer gain from the standpoint of the Scottish Episcopal bishops.

21

Ecumenical Prospects

THE last two chapters have shown us two of the assets enjoyed by the Anglicans and their Ecumenical fellow-travellers in the drive to take over the Church of Scotland. English nationalism has always been an immensely powerful force which has been able to profit by the disloyalty syndrome which is a perennial feature of Scottish history. Chapters 18 and 19 provide us with excellent evidence for transposing this statement of Anglo-Scottish power ratios into contemporary ecclesiastical terms. The Anglican move to reconstitute the Church of Scotland on lines approved by Canterbury is a very formidable drive which can count on the existence of a considerable Anglican fifth column within the Church of Scotland. And in Chapter 20 we saw that the Scottish Episcopal bishops have very good sociological reasons for securing union (naturally on their own terms) with the Church of Scotland, and that through their influence on the Edinburgh Establishment they are in a position to exert pressure on Kirk ministers who wish to stand well with that Establishment.

This does not exhaust the Ecumenical party assets. The Ecumenicals have developed, no doubt quite unconsciously, the technique of loaded prayer. It is a striking instance of the degree to which the Ecumenicals have divided the Church that they have introduced their fellow Christians to the experience of being prayed against. The experience is a rather shattering one. To hear an Ecumenical party leader whom one personally respects pray a prayer of the variety: 'O Lord, who knowest that it is only sin that keeps us apart, take away the evil that prevents us from being one with our Anglican brethren' is not a light matter. For his prayer would at least in part be answered by one's own immediate demise through a heart seizure.

The technique of the loaded prayer has enabled the Ecumenicals to harness the devotional life to party ends. It is interesting at a conference in an Ecumenical centre to notice prayers of the type: 'We pray for the Methodist Church. Hear us, O Lord, as we pray for our Methodist brethren. We pray for those of them who have been moved by the Holy Spirit to hear the call of faith and to go forward into union with the Anglican Church. And we pray for those of them who are holding back through misunderstanding or prejudice. May they too be moved by The Spirit to hear and answer the call of faith. . . .' A prayer of this kind would arouse no adverse comment at an Ecumenical conference. The setting up of Ecumenical centres, to which church groups can be invited and where the devotional life can be transformed into an instrument of party propaganda, is obviously a potent weapon in the hands of the Ecumenical party.

Another asset of the Ecumenical party in the Church of Scotland is political skill, the ability to get committees with the right majorities and the right conveners and at the same time to preserve a façade of impartiality by having a few well-known non-Ecumenicals as a powerless minority. Any vacant places can then be filled by a few plain modest men from remoter Scotland who can be relied on either to be impressed by ecclesiastical top brass or at least not to be present too often in the winter snows. With a place or two reserved for the ecclesiastics whose sole principle is always to be on the winning side, the formula is completed and so far has paid off handsomely.

The Ecumenical party started off as a pocket of eccentricity in the Church of Scotland. It has been the tolerant practice of that Church to turn such pockets, whether Ecumenicals, teetotalers or liturgical enthusiasts, into Assembly Committees. The reports and deliverances which such committees bring forward are again listened to by the Assembly with a great deal of tolerance, however off-centre they are. The reason for this apparently rather complacent tolerance is that everyone knew that with the Barrier Act[1] being what it is, for the Assembly to listen to these reports and approve these deliverances won't do much harm to anybody anyway.

From such a harmless place in the scheme of things the Ecumenical party moved to a much more powerful one. By December 1966 it had almost reached the position where the wary ecclesiastic, ambitious about his future, would be careful not to criticise its proposals publicly. Further, as the *Scottish Daily Express* has pointed out, the Ecumenical controls some vitally important committees. It controls the Inter-Church Relations Committee,[2] and the Panel on Doctrine. The way in which they secured control of the latter body is illustrative of Ecumenical politics. When the Panel on Doctrine was set up it was stated explicitly that it was not meant to be a device to enable one school of thought to enforce its will on the whole Church. To avoid this certain safeguards were written into its membership. The most important of these was a provision whereby the professional theologians on the Panel representing the four Scottish Divinity Faculties, should serve on it for four years only. Abolition of this provision was agreed to by a later Assembly which did not see its significance. Protest against this by the Glasgow Divinity Faculty was ignored. As a result, Ecumenical party professors have been able to stay on the Panel indefinitely. The inevitable implication of Professor Cheyne's admirably clear article on the Panel on Doctrine[3] is that this panel sends down to Presbyteries the interpretations of Church of Scotland doctrine and constitution most acceptable to Lambeth. Its secretary is Mr. Muirhead whose proposal for episcopal ordination forms one of the central features of the Grey Document.

An almost equally important committee held by the Ecumenicals seems to have been the Nomination Committee of the Assembly of 1966 (despite its non-Ecumenical convener). This can be seen from the new delegation which the Nomination Committee has chosen to talk with Anglicans in the new phase

1. See p. 177.
2. A typical manifesto of this Committee is quoted on p. 118.
3. Printed in New College Bulletin.

of discussions now opening. Two non-Ecumenicals, Mr. Andrew Herron and Mr. Jarvie are on this new body. As respectively the convener of the Nomination Committee and the mover of the Anti-Ecumenical motion in the Assembly the claims of these two gentlemen were hard to resist. Together they provide the representative façade of the powerless non-Ecumenical party minority which is a feature of Church of Scotland delegations to talk with Anglicans. Over against them is the solid Ecumenical party core of Dr. Dougall, Messrs. Barbour and Muirhead and Michael, all four of them members of the Regional Group which produced the Grey Document. The Convener is Professor J. K. S. Reid, a delegate to the Nottingham Conference calling for one church for Scotland in 1980, a former vice-convener of the Inter-Church Relations Committee and a member of the Panel on Doctrine, neither of them bodies with an anti-Ecumenical party slant. The composition of the new committee must have given a fair degree of satisfaction to the Anglicans. As one Assembly wag is reported to have said, this was an occasion for the Kirk to send a dove of peace to the Episcopalians but it was hardly necessary to send a whole covey of Mother Carey's chickens.

In the light of the actions of similarly composed committees in the past, there is little difficulty in forecasting what this one will do. The Craig Committee signed the Bishops' Report, the Dougall Committee sent the Grey Document to the Holland House Conference. Can there be any doubt that this new committee will sign a third capitulation to Anglican imperialism? It will bring this to the Assembly and to the Presbyteries for ratification under the Barrier Act. For the third time in fifteen or twenty years the Church of Scotland will be distracted from its task of evangelisation and meeting the challenge of secularism in order to be plunged into a nation wide acrimonious and loveless controversy. For the third time the Church of England, thanks to the superior skill and loyalty of its diplomats and their unyielding imperialist policy, will go unscathed. This time the Church of England does not even have to carry out the pretence of negotiating with the Church of Scotland. The Kirk's surrender on this occasion is to be made to the Church of England's numerically insignificant satellite in Scotland.

Yet another asset of the Ecumenical is that the power equations of Inter-Church relations are in his favour. Thus the rising ecclesiastic in any of the British churches is bound to attack this book. A work like this must be assailed. For it shows that the non-Ecumenical is that vicious animal who defends himself when attacked. After having been told ever since the Bishops' Report that he is against the Will of God, Christ and the Holy Spirit, and that anything he does is Satan manoeuvring into position, the non-Ecumenical has had the impertinence to criticise back in this book.

In particular the rising young ecclesiastic in any of the non-Roman British churches should be sure to attack this book. The power equations demand that he do this. The Establishment of his church look up to the Establishment of the Church of England. You may well have seen a Church of Scotland or an English non-conformist church leader at a social gathering, hovering round a Church of England bishop with short quick steps, desperate to get a chance of saying a few words to the great man. You will not have seen the hovering process in reverse.

Now this book has contained criticisms of Anglican bishops. The rising young ecclesiastic must attack it. Do not let him be discouraged. Reasoned argument is not necessary. Just be in the twentieth century, follow the *New Christian,* choose a bunch of strong epithets and level them at the book. Or follow the Bishop of Bristol, the Convener of the Church of England Committee for Ecumenical Discussion with the Church of Scotland. What better example could you get and what did the Bishop say in the Convocation of Canterbury about the *Scottish Daily Express* whose Editor happens to be a Church of Scotland elder. The bishop's words were that this newspaper 'had vitiated all discussion and still does so by shrill vituperation and gross distortion.' That is a well rounded phrase to use in the Ecumenical dialogue and help on the healing of the body of Christ. Our rising young ecclesiastic could well use a similar one against this book. He doesn't even need to read the book to do this. Quite a number of Ecumenicals who attack the *Scottish Daily Express* boast that they never read the rag—though to be sure the Bishop of Bristol did on the morning the Holland House Conference began.

But there are unmistakeable signs that the Ecumenicals' constant professions of enthusiasm for and identification of their policy with the Holy Spirit and the will of God are beginning to arouse a certain nausea. In the January 1966 television dialogue Dr. Whitley refused to accept Mr. Muirhead's invocation of the Holy Spirit, and suggested that the third person of the Trinity was being used to cover one or two rather doubtful features of Ecumenical party policy. This could have devastating consequences. Newspapermen hitherto reluctant to criticise Ecumenical party policy because they were averse to criticising the Divine Will might take a different line now that the suspicion is arising that the two things are not necessarily identical. It will perhaps be a little harder to sell the Ecumenical line even to papers other than the *Scottish Daily Express*.

22

Decision for the Non-Ecumenical

IT is time now to take a look and try and anticipate as far as we can the final outcome of the events we have been describing. There is no sign that the Anglicans have the slightest compunction about the rancour and havoc that their imperialist demands cause in the Churches who are foolish enough to negotiate with them. We have seen that the present Kirk Committee to talk to the Anglicans is roughly similar in its party alignment to the two preceding ones. Its strong pro-Anglican core will insist that the terms for a surrender to Anglican demands are proposed by the Committee to the General Assembly and the Presbyteries in a year or so. This time there will be no need for a Holland House Affair.

What will happen then if the Reid Committee along with perhaps a minority report signed by two or three of its members, brings to the Assembly and Presbyteries a successor to the Bishops Report and the Grey Document, a third scheme for an Anglican take-over bid? No man knows. The third plan for an Anglican take-over bid may be defeated. It is more likely to be defeated in the Presbyteries than in the Assembly. In the Assembly, the Ecumenical party up to January 1966 had gone a long way toward winning the Establishment. But an Assembly majority is not enough for an amendment to the Constitution of the Church of Scotland. In terms of the Barrier Act such an amendment must then go to the Presbyteries. Here the Constitution of the Church of Scotland resembles that of the United States. In deciding for or against a constitutional amendment, the state of New York has one vote and the state of Nevada has one vote. In a similar situation in the Church of Scotland the Presbytery of Edinburgh has one vote and the Presbytery of Lewis has one vote. The Ecumenical party is concentrated in Edinburgh where the Edinburgh Establishment with its basic doctrine that English institutions are U and Scottish institutions are non-U, naturally favours the Episcopal Church. The geographical situation of the Island of Lewis however makes it uncongenial to Establishments of any kind, its Episcopalian population is so scanty as to make a surrender to Episcopacy senseless and the phrase 'English institutions are U and Scottish Institutions are non-U' is probably untranslateable into Gaelic.

The chances of an Anglican take-over bid getting through the presbyteries are rather less than its chance of getting through the Assembly. If it succeeds in gaining a majority in the Assembly and among the Presbyteries, an appeal will almost certainly be made to the Civil Courts. For the Presbyterian Constitution of the Church of Scotland is written into the legislation of the Treaty of Union which has some claim to be considered as the Constitutional Law of Scotland.

There is therefore a chance that any proposals put forward by the Reid Committee for an Anglican take-over bid may be defeated. If so, the General Assembly by its appointment of that committee will have been indulging in brinkmanship of the most dangerous order, a kind of brinkmanship which even at the present moment is highly unsettling and detrimental to the Church's task of evangelisation. But supposing a proposal from the Reid Committee for a reconstitution of the Church of Scotland on lines acceptable to Lambeth does go through the necessary courts, what is the non-Ecumenical to do? This is a question which the present writer has found it almost impossible to get Ecumenical party members even to consider. In fairness to them, they can hardly be expected to concern themselves about the fate of those they consider to be opposed to the will of God and the Holy Spirit. But to the non-Ecumenical that question of what he is to do in the event of an Ecumenical victory in Assembly, Presbytery and Civil Court is an acute one.

'It has become more acute since the Holland House Affair has shown that the Ecumenical party is prepared to buy a speedy

surrender to the Anglican imperialism even at the cost of dis-
obeying Assembly orders. It is obvious that for the non-Ecumenical the time could be fairly near when he has to decide
whether he has to leave a Church which has departed from the
principles it held when he entered it. This decision will only
have to be taken within the Church of Scotland. The superior
skill and loyalty of the Anglican negotiators will ensure that it
does not have to be taken by any Anglican.

It is obvious that this kind of decision to secede or not is both a
grave and a personal one. It is a situation where the individual
must try to face all the implications involved and reach a
decision which enables him to meet the demands of his own
conscience and reach an inner integrity. The present writer in
outlining the factors which will weigh with him in the event of
reconstitution of the Kirk on lines acceptable to Lambeth has
no desire to be dogmatic. Other non-Ecumenicals may think
and act differently. But it is only fair that the ordinary Kirk
member who is kept ignorant of so much in ecclesiastical
diplomacy should know at least one reaction to an Anglican
take-over bid.

To be taken over by Anglicanism means having to accept
both bishops and the myth by which bishops justify their
power, the so-called doctrine of Apostolic Succession. It is often
assumed that to say anything against having a church run by
bishops is old-fashioned and prejudiced. This is not self-evident.
Perhaps the most penetrating thing about bishops has been said
by the contemporary novelist, Iris Murdoch. Of her bishop in
The Bell she writes 'with the affable leisureness of the great
personage who knows that whenever and wherever he arrives he
is immediately the centre of the scene.' Whether it is good for
any Christian to have that assurance is doubtful. Whether it is
good for other clergymen to have bishops is at least arguable.
Bishops have power. It cannot be wise for the sake of one's
wife and family to oppose them too much. In a Presbytery of
the present Church of Scotland presided over by a temporary
Moderator, there is a great deal of plain speaking and not much
respect of persons. In a Presbytery presided over by a permanent Bishop there would be much less plain speaking and much

more respect of persons. It would be much more like a Scottish University Senate, presided over by a permanent Principal. And that, in the view of one who has had a fair experience of both, is a very different body from the present Church of Scotland presbytery.

Bishops are difficult to accept. What is impossible to accept is the doctrine of Apostolic Succession, the device that bishops use to bolster up their power. The power mythos is an old trick. When a privileged class govern a country to suit their own ends they call their rule an aristocracy, government by the best. When Charles I wanted to get his own way, he very naturally believed in the Divine Right of Kings. That way he could sell the idea that anyone who disobeyed him, disobeyed God. No secular monarch to-day would try to get away with the claim 'Le bon Dieu, c'est moi'. But bishops still try to get away with the claim that they alone are the successors of the Apostles of Jesus Christ. The advantages of their believing this and getting other people to believe it are obvious. One should qualify this by saying they are obvious to those who do not deliberately shut their eyes to the part power plays in ecclesiastical life.

Now it is possible to be tolerant of the faded power myths of yesterday. No sensible person worries if a good representative of an old family is called a real aristocrat. But the Christian cannot allow a power myth to contradict such insights as he has of divine grace in action. Spiritually we all live by such insights and we dare not relinquish them. If we must choose between one of these insights and a power myth we must reject the latter.

Hochhuth, in his play, *Der Stellvertreter*, puts such a choice to his audience. It is the choice between the Pope who did not protest when the S.S. commander rounded up the Rome Jews for extermination, and the simple priest who takes the place of one Jew on the extermination train. Which of these two, Hochhuth is asking, is the Stellvertreter, the representative of Christ? Catholics will query whether Hochhuth was fair to the Pope and whether the choice is as stark as he makes it. But Hochhuth is surely right in pointing to the Nazi apocalypse of evil and the lurid light which brings out the contrast between the power myth and the realities of Divine Grace. Certainly both the situations which make it possible for me to accept church union on Anglican terms come from that background.

The English Captain Best has told of the morning when Dietrich Bonhoeffer after holding a short service was taken to execution. Supposing that at that service Bonhoeffer had celebrated Communion and invited Best (whom I am assuming is an Anglican) to partake. Should Best have taken Communion from Bonhoeffer? There are those Anglicans who would say that he should not. I do not wish to criticise them in any way or to doubt the sincerity of their view. But I do not think they and I should be in the same church. We differ too radically on the nature of divine grace.

Some years after the war I was lecturing at a theological course for British Army Chaplains. As it happened they were all Anglicans and I was neither asked nor did I seek to go to their services of Holy Communion. But also present was a Norwegian Army Chaplain and having seen him go to the Communion Services, I was moved one afternoon to ask him 'How come you go to Communion with these English boys when you Norwegians do not have the Apostolic Succession?' The Norwegian put his head back and laughed. Then he told me his story. He had finished this theological studies in the early 1940's. But by that time Bishop Berggrav was locked up by the Gestapo and he could not be ordained. Undeterred the young Norwegian put on skis and escaped over the mountains into neutral Sweden and there he was ordained by a Swedish bishop. Because he was not ordained by one of the greatest of twentieth century Christians, the Anglicans at the Chaplains' course could invite him to Holy Communion and indeed receive it from him. Now I may be wrong, but I don't think God thinks like these Anglicans. I don't think God is a bloody fool.

I trust the two incidents which weigh with me have made it clear that the factors which in the last resort separate me from the Anglicans are not nationalism English or Scottish or being in or out of the twentieth century. They are theological and they are sufficiently great as to leave me no option. If the Anglicans take over my church and they may do so in a year or two they take it over *ohne mich*, without me.

After secession what? Again I do not speak dogmatically but it seems to me that the dignified and magnanimous thing is to concede victory to the Ecumenicals, to let them realise their blueprint for Scotland. That blueprint is contained in the Nottingham Declaration which lays down that by 1980 there is to be One Church in Scotland. We know what Church it is— it is the church which the Ecumenicals have constructed to suit the requirements of their Episcopalian friends. If the Reid Committee brings on a third successor to the Bishops' Report and the Grey Document and gets it through Assembly and Presbytery and possibly through the civil courts, then the non-Ecumenical must concede defeat. He must not be undignified to try and construct a second Church against the wishes of the Ecumenicals. He must let them have their way. He must allow the Ecumenicals to construct their One Church which is closed to all who cannot accept the over-beliefs of 56,000 Scottish Episcopalians. He must let them exclude him from the ordinances of the Christian religion. He must live without the Christian sacraments and die without Christian burial.

23

Conditions of Recovery

Is there any hope for the Church of Scotland or have the Anglicans and their Ecumenical Party fellow travellers wrecked it irretrievably? They have introduced into it a discord infinitely greater than that which existed between any two churches in twentieth century England or Scotland. On the one hand there are the Ecumenicals who believe that their party policy is the Will of God and accordingly that those who oppose it are against Christ. On the other hand there are the non-Ecumenicals who see that the Ecumenicals' declared aim of setting up a church framed to suit the demands of the Scottish Episcopal bishops as the one Church in Scotland involves their own exclusion from Christian ordinances and who have therefore the very strongest motive for resisting it.

There are several reasons why this appalling situation has arisen. One is that the Ecumenical Party, with whom reasoned thought has always played a minor part in comparison with the seizing of convenerships and committee majorities, have failed to reflect on the implications of their party policy. They have failed to see that their Nottingham declaration that there must be˜one Church in Scotland is incompatible with spiritual freedom. With all its faults Scotland is a country where Catholics can find God in the Mass and Free Churchmen can find Him in a Highland Communion. The Ecumenicals propose to do away with this happy state of affairs by 1980. They propose to do this at a time when the Catholic Church, all honour to it, is concerned that men must be allowed to follow their conscience in religious matters. Further the Ecumenical party members do not think of, or still worse, do not care for the many among their fellow Church of Scotland members who may find it difficult to believe in God but who find it impossible to believe in bishops. For the sake of giving their friends, the Scottish Episcopal Church bishops, a social lift up the Ecumenicals are prepared to deprive their fellow church members of the ordinances of the Christian religion.

A second reason for the present acute crisis in the Church of Scotland is that up to the present no one seems to have grasped one fact which the earlier chapters of this book have tried to point out. This is the fact that any party within the Church of Scotland which has identified its party policy with the Will of God has brought disunion and catastrophe on the Church. Any party, whether it calls itself Ecumenical or Evangelical, which does this is using the Will of God as a device in ecclesiastical politics whose function is to cover doubtful party activities and promote lovelessness.

The third and over-riding reason for the present grave situation in the Church of Scotland is of course the diplomatic activity of Anglican imperialism. The Church of England bishops can only abuse the *Scottish Daily Express*, they cannot refute its account of the diplomacy of their church. In negotiation with another church, the Anglican diplomats make no concessions and so spare their own church any dissension. Using the Holy Communion as a bargaining counter the Anglicans force the other church to make sweeping concessions involving a complete reconstruction of its power structure. This they know will arouse a bitter and acrimonious civil war in the other church. But this does not worry the Anglicans, who rely on their fifth column in the other church to win the civil war. Only occasionally, as in the recent attacks on the *Scottish Daily Express* in the Convocation of Canterbury, do the Church of England leaders come out into the open to help their fellow travellers.

This type of inter-church diplomacy is obviously quite painless for the Anglicans and they may be rather proud of it. I think it is quite shocking. Do the Anglicans really think they are helping the cause of Christianity in the present age by going round creating civil wars in other churches?

If the Church of Scotland is to recover from its present intolerable state of inner discord, it must then break off all conversations with the Anglicans for at least twenty-five years. The lesson of the Dougall Committee is that conversations with the Anglicans cannot be rendered safe for the other church by confining them to a number of harmless subjects. The prototype for all such conversations are Lewis Carroll's immortal maritime dialogue with the Anglicans in the role of the Walrus and the Carpenter and the other church in that of the oysters. The subjects proposed for discussion at these seashore conversations by the Walrus were harmless enough but they were irrelevant to their outcome which was terminal for the oysters.

That apart, the Church of Scotland cannot negotiate with Anglicans for the simple reason that in its present acutely divided state, it cannot agree on the personnel of the negotiating committee. The present Reid Committee whose most conspicuous features are a convener who signed the Nottingham declaration and a solid bloc of four members who sent the Grey Document to the Holland House Conference, obviously cannot have the confidence of the whole Church. As long as it continues in existence the unrest and division in the Church of Scotland can only increase.

Cessation of Anglican conversations for twenty-five years is the one hope for the Church of Scotland. Can this be achieved? Only if the vice-like control of the Ecumenical Party over the Inter-Church Relations Committee and the Panel on Doctrine can be relaxed. As the Ecumenicals are adept at holding on to power as well as seizing it, this can only be done through the formation of a second ecclesiastical party. A church with one party is in just as dangerous a state as a country with one party. One of the few signs of hope in 1966 in the Church of Scotland is the rise of the National Church Association. Such a constitutional and loyalist party need be neither negative nor denominational. Its aim, the safeguarding of spiritual freedom in Scotland, is as positive and as vital for the Catholic and the Free Churchman as for anyone in the Church of Scotland.

If twenty-five years respite from Anglican imperialism, can

be secured, how can it be used? First it can be used as a period
for cleansing. Ecumenicity has debased so much that is sacred
in Christianity. We have seen how the Holy Communion has
become a bargaining counter, the Will of God and the Holy
Spirit cover up devices and pretexts for lovelessness, and the
devotional life transformed by the loaded prayer into a means of
ecclesiastical party propaganda. Respite from the Anglican
imperialist drives would enable us to get back to an undebased
spiritual currency.

Then the Church of Scotland could use a respite from Anglican imperialism by getting on with urgent tasks from which it
has been distracted by unceasing Ecumenical party activity.
There is need to consider the framing of new evangelical
strategies in the face of the problems thrown up by the complex
Lowland industrial society on the one hand and the moribund
Highland economy on the other. On the intellectual side there
is need for reassessment in the face of movements like demythologising and secularism. Such movements have to be
scrutinised carefully before any judgement can be passed on
how far the Christian can go with them and where he must
part company with them. It is impossible for all these tasks to
be done by men who cannot be sure when some smart manoeuvre of the Ecumenical party or some snap Assembly decision
will mean that from henceforth there is no room for them within
the Christian Church.

The respite would be an immense boon to a real Ecumenicity.
For it would mean that the Church of Scotland could give up
its Anglican fixation and take seriously the two churches,
which each in its own part of Scotland counts for immensely
more than the handful of Scottish Episcopalians to be found
there.

In the industrial Lowlands, where Scotsmen who may never
have met a Scottish Episcopalian can live in a community
which is nearly 50 per cent Catholic, the situation has been
transformed in recent years. It has been transformed by the
utterances of the Abbot of Nunraw with his insistence that it is
Our Lord's command that Catholic and Protestant Love
one another and by the new Catholic stress that men must be

allowed to follow their conscience in religious matters. Here is a statement of the Will of God that one can respect, utterly different from the shoddy, love-destroying device of ecclesiastical politics which the Will of God has become in conversations with the Anglicans. For it is a return to the Biblical position that what God requires of a man is love and truth in the inward parts.

Doctrinal differences between the Catholics and the Church of Scotland remain and will remain for a long time. But even the differences are respectable. The discussion between the two churches is a theological one. In it no part is played by the insistent but unproved and theologically irrelevant dogma which dominates and vitiates Anglican-Scottish ecclesiastical discussion, the dogma that English institutions are U and Scottish institutions are non-U.

Even if we leave aside dogma, co-operation with the Catholics could bring about a result far more socially valuable than anything to be achieved by negotiation with the Episcopalians. If the Catholic Church in Scotland and the Church of Scotland could reach an agreed statement on Christian ethics, such a step would be at least one salutary measure against the lawlessness which is far too prevalent in some parts of Scotland today.

So with the other important church in Scotland today, to which in some parts of the North-West the Church of Scotland stands in the relation of a minority church. The Free Church of Scotland does not contain any of the Scottish upper classes and the Edinburgh Establishment will not put any pressure on the Ecumenical party to enter into a Binding Covenant with it. It is in fact the church of a defeated civilisation. That accounts for a lot in it. It accounts for the austere grandeur of some of its services, where anyone with any sense of the numinous can detect that God is near. It accounts for the things with which the Free Church is identified in the Lowlands and England, Sabbatarianism, a rigid Calvinism and a fundamentalist form of Biblical interpretation. None of these things existed in the North-West before the end of its civilisation, as can be confirmed by anyone who cares to take a look at contemporary records.[1] It is shallow and loveless to criticise these aspects of Free Church religious life. It is much better to recognise that a people who are defeated in this world must hold on to the next one with a vice-like grip. If Ecumenicals really wish for better relations with all Churches in Scotland and not just with one that has a social cachet and if, as they boast, they are not afraid of what is costly, then let them go all out and rebuild the Highland economy. After twenty-five years of that kind of effort the difference between Church of Scotland and Free Church Biblical interpretation would have decreased markedly. It is just not true to think that Biblical interpretation is un-affected by economic, political or military factors. The German example shows that. Bultmann's anti-Nazi record is impecca-ble. But in the years of Nazi persecution, the Confessional Church minister's Biblical interpretation was a near-funda-mentalism. 'Es steht geschrieben'—'it is written' was his answer to every question. A few short years later Bultmann's radical Biblical criticism was a burning issue in Germany. But only after General Eisenhower's armies had liberated Western Germany. Probably any church in a situation of crisis reverts to something as near fundamentalism as makes no odds. The first and very costly step for Ecumenicity in the North-West is to get Highland civilisation out of its state of chronic crisis.

This raises a further point at which a twenty-five years respite from Anglican imperialism would be an immense benefit to Ecumenicity. It would give time for real thought which up till now has had to take a second place to ecclesiastical politics. The tempo of Ecumenicity has been set by the time-table of Anglican imperialism. Scotland, the soft underbelly of Protest-antism, has to be tackled immediately after the absorption of Methodism and before the immensely hard task of the extinc-tion of Protestantism in America and Europe and its replace-ment by Anglicanism is begun. In Scotland the Anglicans and the Kirk's Ecumenicals who do their bidding, have not had

1. Cf. Elizabeth Grant of Rothiemurchus, *Memoirs of a Highland Lady*, p. 143. 'There was no very deep religious feeling in the Highlands up to this time (1812). The Shorter Catechism and the fairy stories were mixed up together to form the innermost faith of the Highlander, a much gayer and less metaphysical character than his Saxon-minded countrymen.

much time. Often in talking with Ecumenicals one has had the feeling that they were not really listening but were looking over their shoulder at what for them as the more urgent task of securing the right conveners and the right committee majorities. The haste has always been intensified by the fact that some of the most distinguished of the Ecumenical leaders have been oldish men obviously anxious to achieve a final settlement of Anglo-Scottish ecclesiastical problems before they die. It is, alas, not so easy as that. But the stress on haste has been detrimental to thought. This is accentuated by the fact that in the nature of the case the function of Ecumenical language is to disguise the crudities of Anglican imperialism. Thus the Grey Document alters the proposed 'recognition' of present Church of Scotland ministers to 'acceptance' of them. The change of word seems harmless enough. Only someone versed in Ecumenical language realises that it means that the Scottish Episcopalians are not, even after the Binding Covenant, going to recognise the present ministers of the Church of Scotland as proper minister, but simply to accept them as one accepts unavoidable necessities. So the Grey Document says 'all future ordinations would be episcopal-presbyteral and within the succession hitherto formally acknowledged by the Church of the Anglican Communion'. What the document really means is that to make sure that the present type of Church of Scotland minister dies out, all future Church of Scotland ministers must be ordained by an Anglican bishop. But the Grey Document does not say this and so presumably Dr. Dougall was able to say in his extraordinary Assembly reply to Mr. Dale that episcopal ordination of future Kirk ministers was not even discussed at the conversations. Whatever this use of language is, it is not thinking.

A twenty-five year respite from Anglican imperialism, would mean that language in Ecumenical matters would be set free to express thought instead of having the perverted function of concealing action. Ecumenicity desperately needs some good hard thinking. It needs analysis and not just reiteration of its basic concept, the One Church, with a view to ascertaining whether this particular Oneness expresses love and allows for spiritual freedom. It needs examination on such a point as to whether the difference between English theology on the one hand and German and Scottish theology on the other is based on the different impact of Romanticism in the three countries. In England, Romanticism took the admirable form of the Oxford Movement, a revitalisation of the Church and the social concern that we see in Disraeli's novels. In these circumstances it is understandable if English theologians can see the Church embodied in the bishops in Romantic terms as one of Burke's banks of reason which possess more wisdom than the individual. But this attitude to the church and its bishops is impossible in Scotland where Romanticism is best symbolised by Scott's preposterous dressing up of the unfortunate George IV in a kilt and in Germany where Romanticism culminated in the horrors of Nazism. In these two countries theology is much more connected with the Aufklärung.

This suggestion is not put forward dogmatically but as one possible explanation of a feature of English theology we noted earlier. It is only a point worth looking into. But there is no time to look into it if the Ecumenicals adhere to their Nottingham time schedule of everything Anglican by 1980.

Perhaps the most desperate need in thought about Ecumenicity is an honest admission of the fact of power. Churches are power structures, the relations between churches are power relations, apostolic succession is a power mythos, the call for oneness has often been a demand for power, it even can be argued, though not necessarily affirmed, that orthodoxy is the view of those who possess power in the church. Now this is embarrassing for the Christian Church for the Incarnation, the Babe born in a manger, has been depicted in not a few Christian presentations as the supreme example of a surrender of power. Whether this is the reason or not Ecumenical inter-Church conversations never mention that the considerations of power ever sullied an ecclesiastic's mind. On this respect they resemble nothing so much as an interminable symposium on marriage in the course of which no one ever mentions that there is such a thing as a sexual instinct.

Such a treatment of marriage would be an absurd refusal to

mention the obvious and that is exactly what characterises the so-called Ecumenical dialogues. After all, the Pope, who can determine when many millions of men can go to bed with their wives has what for an elderly Italian bachelor clergyman is an extraordinary amount of power. No one who admires the wisdom and insight of the present Pope is going to imagine that power factors are the sole or chief elements in his decision for or against contraceptives. But is it a compliment to the Pope to imagine that these factors are completely absent from his mind in reaching that decision? After all if public opinion polls tell him that even at present an increasing number of Catholics are using contraceptives then to persevere in their prohibition will only invite disobedience and so weaken the power of the Catholic Church. On the other hand, if the Pope admits contraceptives, he gives up all hopes of the United States becoming a Catholic country. It would of course be quite unfair to imply that power factors only weigh with the Pope and the Catholic Church. The presbyterian or congregationalist minister who wants a bishop to quell his troublesome congregation is equally swayed by them.

Ecclesiastics have so far shown no inclination to talk about power as a factor in Church structures and inter-Church relations. Until that is done all talk of the One Church is suspect. For oneness can be the demand of an imperialism like Hitler's which brooks no rival and tolerates no limits. And it can be the demand of an exclusiveness so extreme as to exclude from a ration card or the Christian Sacraments. There is only one way for Christianity to ensure that its oneness is not such an evil oneness but solely the oneness of love. That way is for Christians to insist on spiritual freedom, the right of a man to worship God according to his conscience, the right not to be deprived of the Sacraments and to be browbeaten into believing that he is opposing the will of God if he cannot conscientiously accept the power-myth of apostolic succession.

Spiritual freedom is a necessity for the Christian individual. But it is equally a necessity for a Christian Church to grow as well as to claim. For how else can a Church be sure that it has within itself something of the Incarnation, that supreme surrender of power. The Church which makes an uncritical demand for oneness, whether it be the Church of the Massacre of St. Bartholomew or the Church of the Massacre of Dunaverty, is a Church which worships power rather than the God who laid aside His power to become the child of Bethlehem and the man of Calvary. And that ultimately is why we must reject the Nottingham Declaration which demands One Church for Scotland. Once that declaration is rejected Scotland will again become a country where Christians can love one another and there will be an end both to Ecumenicals denouncing their critics as hostile to God's will and to books like this. For one who has known in bad times and in good the unfailing friendship of Anglicans, it is not pleasant to write of their church leaders as has been done in this book. But politeness can run out when we are dealing with those who threaten us with death, whether physical or spiritual. And Scotland with One Church closed to all who cannot accept the over-beliefs of the Scottish Episcopal Church is a spiritual death, the kind of spiritual death where one cannot go to a country Church with one's children and must live without the Christian Sacraments. Until the threat of that spiritual death is removed one can only say to Anglicans and Ecumenicals the words which a great Englishman once spoke to some earlier Church of Scotland ministers who identified their ecclesiastical politics and the Will of God. His words were 'I beseech you, in the bowels of Christ, think it possible you may be mistaken.'